the japanese spa

A Guide to Japan's Finest Ryokan and Onsen

Akihiko Seki and Elizabeth Heilman Brooke

photography by Akihiko Seki

TUTTLE

contents

Around Tokyo

Gora Kadan　強羅花壇
Tsubaki　海石榴
Atami Sekitei　あたみ石亭
Kona Besso　古奈別荘
Yagyu-no-Sho　柳生の庄
Seiryuso　清流荘
Senjyuan　仙寿庵
Bankyu Ryokan　本家伴久万久旅館
Sanraku　山楽

Kyoto and Nara

Hiiragiya　柊屋
Seikoro Inn　晴鴨樓
Kikusuiro　菊水楼

Central Japan

Ryugon　龍言
Yumoto Choza　湯元長座
Wanosato　倭乃里
Kayotei　かよう亭
Araya Totoan　あらや滔々庵
Houshi　法師

Northern Japan

Mukaitaki　向瀧
Saryo Soen　茶寮宗園
Tsuru-no-Yu　鶴の湯
Kuramure　蔵群

Southern Japan

Sekitei　石亭
Yamatoya Besso　大和屋別荘
Murata　無量塔
Miyazaki Ryokan　宮崎旅館
Yusai　優彩
Gajoen　雅叙苑

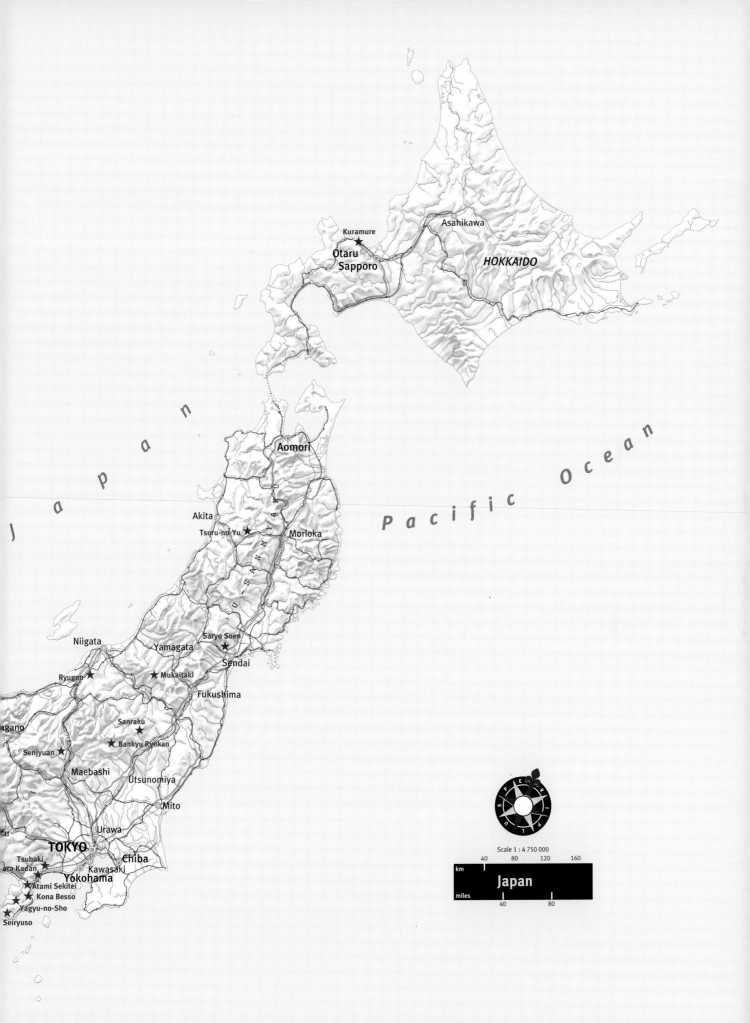

HOKKAIDO

Kuramure ★
Otaru
Sapporo
Asahikawa

Japan

Aomori

Pacific Ocean

Akita
Tsuru-no-Yu ★
Morioka

O-SANMYAKU

Niigata
Yamagata
Saryo Soen ★
Sendai
Ryugon ★
Mukaitaki ★
Fukushima
gano
Sanraku ★
Senjyuan ★
Bankyu Ryokan ★
Maebashi
Utsunomiya
Mito
Urawa
TOKYO
Tsubaki ★
Chiba
ra Kadan ★
Kawasaki
Atami Sekitei ★
Yokohama
Kona Besso ★
Yagyu-no-Sho ★
Seiryuso ★

Scale 1 : 4 750 000

| 40 | 80 | 120 | 160 |
km

miles
| 40 | 80 |

Japan

The Japanese Ryokan: A Timeless Retreat

Slip off your shoes and enter a world that is distinctly Japanese. Cherry blossoms. Zen. Foamy green tea. Warm water meditations one might call, simply, a bath. Hospitality of honor. Ritualized routines to quiet, to sooth the mind, the spirit.

The philosophers, the potters, the tea masters and the poets of Japan, who, thousands of years ago halted the elaborate evolutions of beauty in all its sumptuous gold-leaf manifestations, have attracted generations of humbled aesthetics. Van Gogh, Picasso and Frank Lloyd Wright are among the many painters, architects and creative iconoclasts who have looked to Japan for inspiration. Free spirits have marveled at Japan's studied serenity and heightened awareness of the beauty of a single blade of grass, a single flower petal, a single wave, a single volcanic mountain. They have studied wood, earth and stones, lines, planes and space, and man's daily interaction with the impermanence of nature.

A Japanese Zen monk once described absolute beauty as "pure white snow in a silver dish." This crystalline perception of beauty, the distilled, asymmetrical, modest interpretations of Japanese art and architecture that now are emulated around the world are no longer easy to find in Japan. A 21st century traveler to Tokyo must visually edit telephone wires, construction cranes, a wealth of concrete box buildings, concrete mountain faces, neon, plastic and florid representations of nature in ersatz form.

The good news is that even the Japanese have begun to look for spaces that are authentic, organic, human, historic, refined and natural. There are classic inns throughout Japan that have maintained and refreshed their thatched roofs, their bold wood beams, their fragrant tatami floors. And there are innkeepers, who, thankfully, have saved farmhouses, samurai and lordly residences, sometimes moving them and adapting them to accommodate modern-day guests. There

are also recently built inns that are prize-winning in design, progressive in their reverence for the use of natural materials, old-world traditional in their concern for showing foreign visitors the unique rituals of a night spent at a Japanese inn.

It long has been lamented that Japan is still backward in opening doors and receiving foreign guests in a way that does not offend host and guest alike. That too is changing. The rigid formality, the total inability to communicate in any language other than Japanese and the abstruse dance of shoes and slippers and bowing and bathing costumes are no longer the norm in Japan. At last, selfconscious Japan recognizes that the international community treasures all that is special about Japanese hospitality and culture, yet requires more interpretation to access Japan's less traveled paths. The Japanese government has launched a multi-million-dollar campaign, Yokoso! Japan, to welcome overseas visitors and encourage Japanese innkeepers and restaurateurs to translate some of Japan's mysteries for a wider audience.

With an eye for the beauty of shadow, color and texture, bilingual photographer Akihiko Seki has spent two years traveling Japan in order to select and visually capture his favorite Japanese inns and spas. He has tried to visit each inn with the wide-eyed anticipation of a foreigner, who might speak little Japanese and know little of the context of Japanese inn-keeping and hot spring visiting.

Clockwise from top: Sekitei, across from Miyajima, is a garden of peace overlooking the Inland Sea; Saryo-Soen in Sendai, a boutique ryokan on six-and-a-half acres in the Akiu Onsen region; Edo elements remain alive at Tsuru-no-Yu in Akita, an inn popular with hikers, history buffs and bathers; Tsuru-no-Yu is one of Japan's most refreshingly authentic retreats; Built in 1873, Mukaitaki in Aizu-Wakamatsu makes guests feel like their futon are floating among the trees.

Light-years away from a hotel, a motel, a love hotel, or a capsule hotel, a ryokan is a traditional Japanese inn that can be found nearly anywhere in Japan. Ryokan are most often found in settings of historic significance or luxuriant natural beauty. They have clung to history, architecture, art and ways of doing things, and are thus usually preferred by foreign guests as excellent backdrops for studying and experiencing all that is different about Japan.

Peddlers, couriers, pilgrims and loyal lords to the Tokugawa shogunate of the 17th century were among the first streams of travelers in need of a roof and a hearth for the night. Every other year, *daimyo* ("local lords") were required to verify their commitment to the shogun by presenting themselves in what was then called Edo, Tokyo. Understandably, lodgings along the Tokaido highway linking Kyoto to Tokyo popped up, and soon there was a class system and shogunate regulations for them as well. For court nobles and highly regarded samurai, there were *honjin* with formal gardens, decorated rooms, tatami-covered daises for visiting lords and hidden exits for guests in need of quick escapes from their enemy. *Waki-honjin* and *hatagoya* were for less-esteemed samurai, servants and other wayfarers of the day.

Check-in involved some bowing and tying up of one's horses. Guests usually went into the nearest town for dinner and female "companionship." The Tokugawa shoguns decided that it was time for some regulating of the night

and declared that inns must serve dinner. There went the excuse to prowl around town. So, female courtesans began to bring their demure entertainments to the inns. Breakfast became another inn service, and the tradition of including dinner and breakfast with a night's lodging has remained a unique element of ryokan hospitality to this day.

Depending on the specific ryokan, its heritage or its culinary emphasis, dinner at a Japanese inn can be a highly formal multi-course meal, *kaiseki*, whose origins are from the noble courts of Kyoto, or a simpler country feast of tempura, simmering broths, multigrains and wild mountain vegetables. Japanese breakfast is traditionally protein-rich with grilled fish, sweetened eggs, beans, miso soup, pickles and rice. Today's ryokan are becoming a bit more flexible with timing and presentation of these meals. Many inns now allow guests to specify the time for dinner, and meals can be taken in a separate dining room. A few inns now even allow guests the option of having dinner at a local restaurant.

Sitting like a *daimyo* before a low table and receiving as many as 10, to 12 or even 15 dishes of culinary and artistic craftsmanship over the course of two to three hours is an opportunity to slow down, to savor each mouthful, to appreciate the design, the art and the architecture of a typical ryokan guest room. Many of the design elements of these rooms were originally taken from temple halls. The rooms usually appear quite spacious, because they are devoid of the expected beds, desk, stuffed chair and reading lights. Rooms are open, ready to welcome people. Light is filtered through sliding screens of translucent paper, *shoji*, that are closed for total privacy or opened to reveal gardens, perhaps, forests or mountains, water and sky.

Small recessed wall spaces, *tokonoma*, were also originally developed to serve a temple purpose. These shallow spaces were altars for placing offerings of flowers

Top: Murata, on the east coast of Kyushu at Yufuin Onsen, a "petit" onsen ryokan of century-old farmhouses with open, airy spaces of Western and Eastern comfort.
Below: The Kayotei Inn in Ishikawa offers highly attentive service and Sukiya-style beauty at its most understated elegance.

and incense and for hanging sacred images and venerable scrolls. In today's guest rooms, *tokonoma* are for fresh ikebana blossoms, calligraphy or hand-painted silk scrolls and treasured works of art.

Many preferred ryokan are a mix of the Sukiya and Shoin architectural styles popular in the Edo Period (1615–1868). A *sukiya* is a small wooden tea-ceremony building, whose concept first originated with the tea cottages of the Muromachi Period (1333–1573). Its construction of wood and plaster is simple, in concert with the wonder of nature just beyond the sliding door, which more often that not, comes in the form of an adjacent courtyard garden with rocks and a tree, moss and a stone lantern—a place for meditation.

A *shoin* is a library or private study once used by priests, and then more grandly conceived by feudal warlords in the 16th century as a setting for meeting important people of the day. Rooms are quite big with strong, straight-edged pillars. Tatami mats thick with rice straw and covered in woven rush completely cover the floor. There is the decorative *tokonoma* alcove, *fusuma*, sliding screens, wood-latticed *shoji* windows and *amado*, outer wooden shutters. Behind ornately painted *chodaigame* doors, bodyguards once lurked in wait to protect their lord from possible intruders.

Happily, today's ryokan are dwellings of peace, retreats from the tensions of the wider world. As Mr Seki traveled his homeland, he realized that nearly all his most cherished ryokan were onsen ryokan, ryokan near enough to natural springs to be able to offer guests the joys of a spa. The only exceptions to this soothing coincidence are in Kyoto and Nara, historic capitals of Japan that most travelers wish to see at least once, if not many times. Hopefully, the wealth of preserved history and the magnificent garden design that these cities offer—not to mention the remarkable service and environments of the city inns themselves—offset yearnings for an onsen bath.

The numerous active volcanoes in the archipelago of Japan bring with them the agreeable geological phenomenon of over 2,500 sources of healing waters. However, these waters have to pass certain regulations before they can be used as "onsen" waters. As defined by the Japanese Hot Spring Law, onsen waters must flow from underground to the surface at over 75 degrees Fahrenheit, and contain a minimum amount of minerals such as iron or manganese, sodium or sulfur.

The Japanese passion for the bath may date to ancient farmers stepping into bubbling open-air pools to wash away sweat and grime from a day's labor, or to the Shinto and Buddhist tenets that dignify hot soaks. Ritual cleansing and purification are Shinto practices. A key tenet in Buddhism, bathing "removes seven ills and bestows seven blessings." It is thought that mineral water bathing may aid rheumatism, arteriosclerosis, gout and skin disease and is, undoubtedly, a cure for exhaustion.

On the assumption that most travelers fly into Tokyo, the first ryokan presented are within a two- to three-hour Shinkansen ("bullet train") ride of the capital. For those fortunate enough to be able to further explore, ryokan at the end of roads far to the north or far to the south are so very pleasing they often become personal favorites.

According to Zen wisdom, "The journey is the destination." Along the way, these Japanese spas help us to remember just that.

Clockwise from top: At Houshi in Komatsu there is a special garden villa of exclusive privacy; Hiiragiya in Kyoto offers the tranquility of old Japan—some rooms are over 100 years old; Saryo Soen in northern Japan is one the top onsen ryokan in all of Japan; Ryugon in Niigata showcases samurai homes distinctly decorated with calligraphy scrolls and spaces of museum-caliber craft and construction; Some rooms in Gora Kadan in Hakone have low tatami beds, all are serene in lighting, minimalist in design.

Ryokan and Onsen Etiquette: Essential Knowledge

Time, experiences, relationships—these are precious. Time in a Japanese inn does not beat to high-speed rhythms. Is that not why ryokan time appeals? The rich experience of truly feeling one with Japanese-style living, even for a night and a day, is rare and yes, very different. Interacting with hosts and fellow inn guests takes the meaning of international understanding to a personal level. The more guests know of ryokan and onsen expectations and customs, the more they can feel at ease. Allow these particular Japanese customs to suavely coax all who cross the threshold, who slip into steamy hot spring waters to pause…to relinquish distracting concerns…to delight in the many exquisite facets of a Japanese spa inn. Herewith, essential truths of some ryokan and onsen rituals:

If you are not fluent in Japanese, it is preferable to fax or e-mail your reservation request. English is more readily understood in writing than on the phone. You can expect to receive a written response. Keep in mind that for the most part, English is little understood. Unless we have specifically stated here that an innkeeper is fluent, you should expect to be trying to speak Japanese.

The New Year (January 1–3), Golden Week (April 29–May 5), and Obon (August 13–15) are Japan's highest travel seasons. Expect to pay maximum rates, and be aware that rooms are often booked more than a year in advance for these popular times.

Since a night in a ryokan includes a set dinner and breakfast, rates are per person and not by room. Usually, service charges are included in the rate, but some ryokan charge an additional 10 to 15 percent. A five percent consumption tax and a bathing tax of ¥150 per person will be added to your bill.

Personal checks are not popular in Japan and are rarely accepted by ryokan. Most ryokan accept major credit cards, but it is wise to confirm acceptable means of payment when making reservations.

Tipping is generally not customary in Japan, but if you wish to express appreciation for unusually attentive hospitality and room service provided by your *nakai-san* ("maid") upon departure, you can present ¥2,000–3,000 in a small envelope.

A *nakai-san* is the specific hostess assigned to care for you during your stay. Upon arrival, you are likely to be welcomed by the *nakai-san* and guided to your room. She will help you fill out the hotel register. She may serve you tea and a sweet bun, and—depending on the ryokan—serve you dinner and breakfast. She will explain where dinner will be served and may ask if you have a time preference. At some point during the evening, she will return to your room to pull out the futon (one or two floor mattresses and a cover quilt) for sleeping. Traditional Japanese pillows are filled with buckwheat husks.

Check-in is usually around 2:00 or 3:00 pm, and it is best to arrive before 4:00 pm, if you would like to follow Japanese custom and enjoy a spa bath before dinner.

At the inn entrance (*genkan*) you will find slippers for you to use during your stay. You should leave your shoes in the entryway and use slippers within the inn. Remove your slippers before stepping on fragile tatami floors, and use the special bathroom slippers, when provided. Try to avoid the comedy of being spied in your bathroom slippers outside of the bathroom! If you decide to take a stroll in the garden, use the *zori* or *geta* thoughtfully provided for you.

Clockwise from top: Gajoen in southern Japan, with enchanting bathtub views of the mountains; Kuramure in northern Japan, a gallery-like ryokan of contemporary art and design, for healing, bathing, refined dining and fun; Yusai—Kurokawa hot spring waters in a Japanese cypress tub; Senjyuan in Minakami has picture windows that showcase the grays, the greens, the grasses beyond the mist of onsen baths; The luxurious Yusai Onsen, in western Kyushu, must be one of the most dramatically stunning in all of Japan.

Leave your in-house slippers beside the garden door and slip on Japanese outdoor footwear.

A typical Japanese-style room will come with a *tokonoma*, an alcove display for flowers and treasured works of art. This seemingly empty space is considered sacred and is, therefore, not a spot to sit or stash your bags. Each guest is supplied with a *yukata*, an informal cotton kimono, and a *haori* or *tanzen*, short robes often made of silk stripes. *Yukata*, *haori* and *tanzen* are to be worn anywhere within the inn, and *yukata* may also be used as pajamas. Tie your *yukata* with the left collar on the top. Buddhist tradition stipulates that the right flap only appears on top when a person is dead.

Onsen are often open all day and night, although they may be closed for mid-morning cleaning. The frequency with which you take to the baths is up to you. It is not uncommon to visit the baths before dinner, after dinner, late in the evening, after drinks in the bar, and before or after breakfast.

You may think you know, but here is "how" to take a bath: don your *yukata* and feel free to bring a small cosmetics bag of preferred toiletries, shampoo, comb or brush. Generic brands of shampoo and body wash are usually provided. Bring along the towel or towels provided in your room. Men and women's baths are most often segregated, and entrances are usually labeled in different colors. In the changing room, place your *yukata* in one of the baskets. Bring the small towel and any toiletries to the showering area. Before entering the mineral baths, wash your body with the hand-held shower nozzle or bucket (*oke*). Beside the onsen waters there may be a small mineral water bath (*kakeyu*) for pre-washing your body and acclimatizing it to the hot temperatures. Fill a bucket with these waters and splash them over you prior to entering the communal bath. Take the small towel with you into the hot springs area. That scant piece of terrycloth is your only chance of modesty, but it is not to enter the waters. Some people drape the towel over their heads, others set it aside.

Onsen temperatures vary. Waters can be warm and comforting, sometimes very hot. The soothing benefits can be felt after only a few minutes, so feel free to alternate between hot and cooler baths. Since the mineral content of certain waters is particularly good for the skin, it is not considered necessary to bathe or rinse after a final onsen soak.

Some inns have private onsen baths adjoining the rooms or *kazukoburo*, family baths for private use. But communal bathing is as Japanese as the *ukiyo-e* woodblock prints that fascinated and inspired American Impressionist Mary Cassatt. Her now famous "Woman Bathing" is a focused, unselfconscious tribute to a ritual that holds great meaning for the Japanese. Stroking the body with soap, removing a day's dirt and floating in a warm watery buoyant embrace— these are pleasures and spa joys the Japanese continue to hold dear.

Clockwise from top: Guests at Yumoto Choza, situated at the foot of the northern Japanese Alps, can choose to hike, climb or wander in the white birch forests; The quiet grounds of Kikusuiro, the oldest ryokan in Nara, provide an ideal place of rest; Yagyu-no-Sho on the Izu Peninsula is nestled in the thick of a bamboo forest in Shuzenji; Saryo Soen in northern Japan, charms with its garden tea-ceremony cottages with pastoral views; Tsuru-no-Yu in northern Japan is one of the most popular "secret" onsen in all of Japan.

Gora Kadan 強羅花壇　Hakone, Kanagawa

The Eden-like intimacy of bathing among the trees and forests of bamboo where pine alone bear witness. A gentle massage with the purest of aromatic plant oils. Shiatsu or Swedish-trained fingers kneading meridians, opening channels of potential energy, slipping from hot, hot waters to open-air baths—a relief, a release, a spa as the sophisticated and the over-scheduled have come to know and appreciate. Welcome to Gora Kadan.

A member of the exemplary Relais & Chateaux group, Gora Kadan knows how to please guests with the most exacting standards. Set in onsen-rich Hakone National Park, Gora Kadan was originally a resort house for relatives of the Imperial family. In 1952 it became a public ryokan, and in 1989, its main building, a luxurious triumph of bamboo, stone, tile and native woods, was built by a series of prominent architects. Its spa, called Kako, or "Fragrance of Flowers," is housed in a traditional Japanese villa and provides facials, revitalizing cellular body treatments using Swiss herbs, and therapies using salt from the Dead Sea. The inn's chief of guest relations greets guests by name and unobtrusively reminds visiting foreigners of ryokan rites and wrongs.

All of the 37 rooms come with unique bathrooms en suite and mini-bars, and seven rooms have private *rotenburo*. There are two onsen and two *rotenburo* for communal use. The rooms are grand in size, serene in lighting, minimalist in design. Some rooms have low tatami beds; some are pure Japanese with futon, low tables for dining and thin seat cushions (*zabuton*). There is a sky-lit heated indoor swimming pool long enough for many a lap, a Jacuzzi, fitness center, sun deck, conference room, reading room and karaoke bar. The 10- or 11-course feast that is dinner can be taken in one's room or in a private dining room. Coffee and newspaper are room-delivered along with Japanese breakfast overlooking lawns and trees of green.

The town of Gora is approximately 60 miles southwest of Tokyo, a 40-minute Shinkansen ride to Odawara, then a 30-minute drive through the mountains to Gora. This is a very active volcanic area—and here and there steam holes spew sulfur mists. Mount Fuji is nearby. People come to play golf, go fishing or boating on Lake Ashi, hike in the hills of the less famous surrounding mountains, Mount Myojogatake, Mount Sengen and Mount Komagatake (which has a cable car service). The famous Hakone Open-Air Museum featuring the sculptures of Picasso and Henry Moore, among others, is only minutes away, as are several other museums of interest.

Down a stone path, amidst maples red and green, here is a balance of Eastern and Western understanding of the many nuances of the concept, "spa."

Address: 1300 Gora, Hakone-machi, Ashigarashimo-gun, Kanagawa-ken 250-0408, Japan. **Tel:** 81 (0)460 2 3331. **Fax:** 81 (0)460 2 3334. **Website:** www.gorakadan.com. **E-mail:** info@gorakadan.com. **Rooms:** 37. **Access:** 40 min from Tokyo to Odawara Station by Tokaido Shinkansen and 30 min drive to Gora by taxi.

Tsubaki 海石榴 Yugawara, Kanagawa

Camellias in December, plum blossoms in February, cherry in April, and the music of a mountain stream all year round. *Tsubaki* is the Japanese word for "camellia," and on the grounds of this gourmet-restaurant-turned-inn, there are as many as 1,500 lush red and pink camellia trees.

Less than two hours south of Tokyo by train or car, Yugawara and Oku-Yugawara Onsen have been popular destinations since the eighth century. Its thermal waters and relative proximity to Tokyo made it a sensible setting for treating wounded soldiers during the Sino–Japanese War in 1894 and the Russo–Japanese War of 1904. In the 1920s, numerous inns and private *besso* ("villas") were built in this area. Acclaimed Japanese writers, painters and movie producers have made Yugawara their place for creative retreat. Here in this place of peace Taikan Yokoyama painted images of Mount Fuji.

Tsubaki first opened about 25 years ago and is a cherished rest stop known for its exceptional cuisine. The emphasis here is on dining with attentiveness, savoring flavors, making a long evening of *kaiseki* fare with Kyoto flair. Upon arrival, guests are presented with warm towels, fragrant green tea and a little sweet, perhaps, a *yokan* or *azuki* bean jelly. Dinner and breakfast are served in guests' rooms overlooking ponds fed by mountain streams and forests of beech and maple and bamboo.

The parade of delicacies called *kaiseki ryori* comes from the ancient "slow" food origins of the tea ceremony. Each dish is a work of mastery—to see, to smell, to taste. A clear soy broth with floating carrot and fish cake is served in a demure bowl of lacquer. Marinated raw oysters and squid are served on the half shell and in vessels of lime rind. An unusual ceramic piece presents sashimi of *maguru* and squid with an artistic grace note of shredded *daikon*.

Some dishes are so artistically presented that it seems aggressive to destroy their delicate beauty for the indulgence of a tempting bite. The chefs of Tsubaki take such pride in presenting a joyous meal that they will even accommodate guests' possible aversions or allergies. If the thought of some of the freshest tuna sashimi in all of Japan does not make your mouth water, grilled fish or meat can be substituted upon request. There is also a banquet room for entertaining business colleagues or clients.

All 29 rooms are in the Sukiya style of a Japanese tea-ceremony house, lattice-work *shoji* paper doors slide open and close along a corridor. Two rooms have private *rotenburo*. There are also two indoor spring baths and two outdoor baths.

With tangerine orchards and Pacific Ocean views nearby, this is a fond area for hiking. Take a walk in the woods, then, in a garden of pink, enlighten your taste buds.

Address: Oku-Yugawara, Yugawara-cho, Ashigarashimo-gun, Kanagawa-ken 259-0314, Japan. **Tel:** 81 (0)465 63 3333. **Fax:** 81 (0)465 63 6640. **Website:** www.tsubaki.net. **E-mail:** kaiseki@tsubaki.net. **Rooms:** 29. **Access:** 50 min from Tokyo to Atami Station by Tokaido Shinkansen and 10 min to Tsubaki by taxi, or 2 hrs drive from Tokyo to Oku-Yugawara through Tomei Kosoku, Odawara-Atsugi Doro and Manazuru-Doro.

Atami Sekitei あたみ石亭　Atami, Izu Peninsula

Rock and stones exalted. It is said that the beauty of a flower or a tree is quite easy to see and understand. Yet the exquisite nature of a stone requires a state of inner peace. *Sekitei* is a stone pavilion, and this ryokan set in a quiet residential neighborhood of fragile pink weeping cherry blossoms, golden fields of rape and bows of acorn-dotted pine trees overlooking Atami Bay honors stone as sculpture, as protector, as mighty foundation.

This onsen area, a mere 60 miles southwest of Tokyo, less than an hour by bullet train, has long been a favorite weekend refuge for businessmen and families. *Atami* translates as "hot sea," and a tale is told that a geyser used to rain hot waters into the sea, killing fishermen's harvest and endangering their livelihood. Thanks to the prayers of a Buddhist monk, the geyser moved into shore and Atami became famous as a source of hot spring waters.

Originally built in 1952 as an exclusive club of villas with private chefs, Atami Sekitei is now affiliated with the leading South Asian resort chain, the Banyan Tree Group. Every year Japan's Master Go Tournament is held here. Many of Atami Sekitei's 29 rooms have views of a pond colorfully swirling with orange and white carp.

Sakuragaoka-Saryo ("Teahouse on Cherry Blossom Hill") is an annex of the original 10 rooms, all with private hot spring baths. From these rooms it is possible to watch the weekend performances of geisha spinning parasols and dancing on a Noh stage set in the garden. Artistically arranged trays and platters of *kaiseki* delicacies are served in guests' rooms. A broth of *enoki* mushrooms, young bamboo shoots, sweet ginger and finely cut egg cake is served in a gold and China red lacquer bowl. Lobster, sea bream and tuna are features of the sashimi course. A little basket might arrive with fine slivers of lotus root, a few pods of *edamame*, and a gingko

nut under the frilly shade of tiny maple leaves. A slice of strawberry floats in a chilled glass of plum wine.

The mineral waters of Atami attract, but there is also the Atami Castle and the Mokichi Okada Association (MOA) Art Museum to visit. The museum overlooks Atami Bay and houses the rich collection of Mokichi Okada, founder of the World Church of Messianity. In a dramatic modern complex, there are ceramics, lacquerware, a cherished tea jar by Edo artist Ninsei, a screen of "Red and White Plum Trees" by Korin Ogata, woodblock prints by Hiroshige and Hokusai among a collection of as many as 3,500 pieces, only 200 of which are on view at any given time. Collector Okada believed that it was "spiritually elevating" to view great art in an "ideal natural setting."

Atami Sekitei displays nature as art.

Address: 6-17 Wada-cho, Atami-shi, Shizuoka-ken 413-0024, Japan. **Tel:** 81 (0)557 83 2841. **Fax:** 81 (0)557 82 2840. **Website:** www.sekitei.co.jp. **E-mail:** sekitei@sekitei.co.jp. **Rooms:** Sekitei 29, Sakuragaoka-Saryo 10. **Access:** 50 min from Tokyo to Atami Station by Tokaido Shinkansen and 5 min to Sekitei by taxi.

Kona Besso 古奈別荘 Izu-Nagaoka, Izu Peninsula

Stepping-stones slow life's pace. With each stone comes a fresh perspective. Treasuring a moment, a view, a taste, a sensation is what this old-world weekend retreat, Kona Besso, is all about.

For hundreds of years the hot springs in this area of the Izu Peninsula, south of Mount Fuji, have attracted big-city dwellers seeking a cosseting and a release from day-to-day striving. Kona Onsen was founded 1,300 years ago and eventually combined with the waters of Nagaoka Onsen to create the source that now feeds Izu-Nagaoka, a small onsen town of 15,000 people.

In the late 1930s, Kona Besso was built as the second home of a Tokyo entrepreneur. It is set in a quiet residential area, about one-and-a-half hours from Tokyo by Shinkansen and then car ride from Mishima Station. To this day Kona Besso gives the comforting feeling that one is entering a private domain.

There are eight independent villas, all designed in Sukiya teahouse-ceremony style. Rooms are decorated with furniture dating from the 18th and 19th century Edo and Meiji Periods. One of the villas, Atari, was modeled after the Ginkakuji Temple in Kyoto. "The Chrysanthemum Beauty," a highly valued painting by modern *ukiyo-e* artist Kiyokata Kaburagi hangs in one of the villa's rooms. The scent of rice tatami mats, the mysteries of sliding paper screen doors, the use of natural blonde bamboo, soft gray granite and uncluttered space is soothing, beguiling. Life here seems far, far away.

Long, long ago, in the Middle Ages, this area was, in fact, a place of exile. Not far from here, in the early 1600s, the legendary shipwrecked Englishman Will Adams built a boat for the shogun and became immortalized as the fictional adventurer in James Clavell's novel, *Shogun*. This picturesque area was the setting for Yasunari

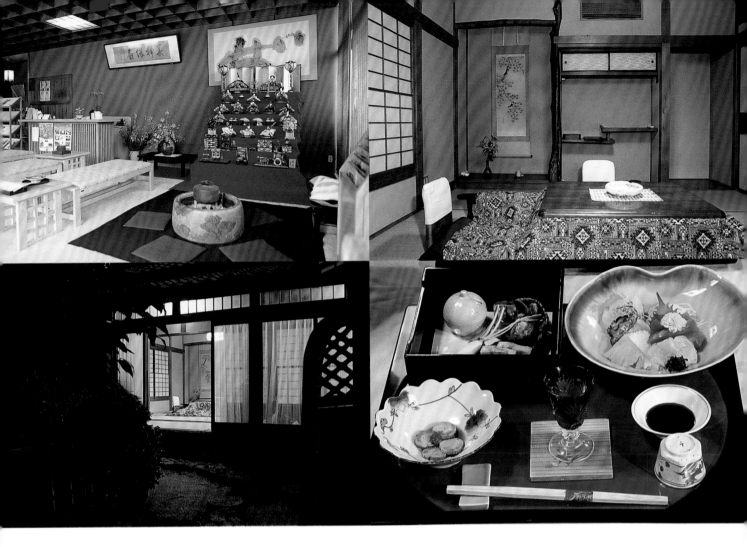

Kawabata's semi-autobiographical novella, *The Izu Dancer*. Kona Besso is still a place of silver pampas grass, of hallowed mountain views, of isolation in a protected and preserved sense. Each of the villas at Kona Besso has its own mineral water bath. There are an additional two communal indoor onsen, one for men and one for women, as well as two al fresco communal baths. On cold nights, hands and toes can also be warmed beneath the quilt of a *kotatsu*, a space heater beneath a table top.

Dinner as well as breakfast are taken in the dining room. Sake or plum wine is served. There is sashimi of tuna, squid and sea urchin. Time stops for conversation and sipping tea.

To experience Kona Besso's lovely weeping cherry blossoms, it is best to book for early April. Tread light, there may be fragile pink beauty beneath that step.

Address: 31 Kona, Izu-Nagaoka-cho, Tagata-gun, Shizuoka-ken 410-0022, Japan. **Tel:** 81 (0)559 48 1225. **Fax:** 81 (0)559 47 1225. **Website:** www.konabesso.com. **Rooms:** 8. **Access:** 1 hr from Tokyo to Mishima by Tokaido Shinkansen and 30 min to Nagaoka by train or by taxi.

Yagyu-no-Sho 柳生の庄　Shuzenji, Izu Peninsula

The beat is of bamboo swords. The music is of a waterfall. Enter the bamboo forest. Feel the samurai spirit. Yagyu-no-Sho is named in honor of an Edo kendo expert, Munenori Yagyu, a highly skilled master of bamboo swordsmanship and strategy.

Ryokan owner Takaya Hasegawa opened Yagyu-no-Sho in 1970 as an exquisite tribute to the hallowed clan, who defended the Tokugawa shoguns from 1603–1867. Mr Hasegawa is himself a master of kendo, trained at the Yagyu-Shinkage school of kendo. Mr Hasegawa's inn, named House of the Yagyu, has a *yagyu-kan*—a "hall for kendo practice," but also for business meetings, parties and artistic Japanese dancing. The setting for the ryokan was specifically selected because it reminded Mr Hasegawa of the original Yagyu's hometown, Yagyu Village in Nara.

In the middle of a bamboo forest in Shuzenji, about two hours by Shinkansen and local train from Tokyo, there are 16 rooms, all in understated Sukiya teahouse style. Tetsuro Okada, considered one of the leading architects of modern Sukiya houses, designed the ryokan. Two rooms, Ume-no-ma and Matsu-no-ma are independent villas with private open-air baths. All of the rooms have private indoor baths of Japanese cypress, fed by springs. There are two communal baths set in the misty woods, one for men and one for women. There are also two communal indoor onsen.

The careful design that magnificently illustrates the power of "less is more" is evident everywhere: along the connecting corridor, airily shielded by a series of latticed screens, at the inn entrance, where a small pond shimmering with carp playfully beckons, before the stone garden path, where a pair of wooden *zori* await naked toes tingling in anticipation of an al fresco stroll in the woods.

In May, the bamboo green forest along the Katsura River is splashed with fuchsia and white azalea blossoms. In autumn the woods are rich with a palette of maple red.

The Kyoto-style *kaiseki* dinners and breakfasts, served in the guests' rooms, also aim to showcase the seasons. Mr Hasegawa formerly managed a Japanese restaurant in Tokyo and thus has a following of wayfarers who are content to merely sample his haute dishes in the seclusion of the forest green. A typical meal might be tofu and baked egg in a broth of mushrooms and shrimp, sashimi of tuna on an exotic lettuce with a sprig of lavender, a gold-brushed box of assorted sushi or a seafood bouillabaisse served in a hollowed-out muskmelon.

English is well understood here, as is the importance of warm hospitality. It is best to book three months in advance. A noble spirit and tranquility await.

Address: 1116-6, Shuzenji, Shuzenji-cho, Tagata-gun, Shizuoka-ken 410-2416, Japan. **Tel:** 81 (0)558 72 4126. **Fax:** 81 (0)558 72 5212. **Website:** www.yagyu-no-sho.com. **E-mail:** info@yagyu-no-sho.com. **Rooms:** 16. **Access:** 1 hr from Tokyo to Mishima Station by Tokaido Shinkansen and 30 min to Shuzenji by train or by taxi.

Seiryuso 清流荘 Shimoda, Izu Peninsula

Kingfishers swerve and dive. Turtles and carp swim in river waters. Oleander, peach and cherry blossoms in their season color the shore. On the banks of the Inouzawa River, there is a splendid resort ryokan, Seiryuso, a house of clear running streams, a house whose hot, hot spring waters flow with abundance.

The natural spring waters flow into Seiryuso at temperatures over 100 degrees Fahrenheit, and are then lowered to a more soothing 88 degrees Fahrenheit. The wealth of water flow is an impressive 550 liters per minute, enough to fully renew the spring waters in the vast 25-meter pool two times a day. To have the space to stretch, to glide, to breathe and move through a spa swimming pool, to contemplatively regard regal palms or meticulously trimmed bushes from the cushy comfort of leather sofas, to dine on beef tenderloin with blueberries and sashimi with wasabi and lime, this spot is not typical in any Japanese or European sense.

Seiryuso is hedonistic in a most refined Japanese manner, an opulent melding of the best of East and West. A member of both The Leading Hotels of the World and Relais & Chateaux, Seiryuso has a helipad, convenient for the 20- to 30-minute hop from Tokyo's Narita Airport. Most guests however travel to Seiryuso and Shimoda via express train, a two-and-a-half hour trip from Tokyo.

A port town on the Izu Peninsula, Shimoda is heavy with historic significance. In 1853, after 265 years of persistent isolation, four black warships led by Commodore Matthew Perry stormed Shimoda Bay and forced the Tokugawa shogunate to enter the unpredictable world of international trade. In 1854, peace talks between Japan and the US reached an amiable close at Ryosenji Temple in Shimoda. Down by the water's edge stands an anchor and black bronze of Perry, and a Black Ship Festival is celebrated every May.

Some travelers may venture to Shimoda for its history and well-preserved *namako-kabe* warehouse architecture, its surf and shaded trails. Still others come to simply soak in its natural thermal waters. Seiryuso, about a 10-minute drive north of Shimoda Station, is a popular retreat for businessmen, artists, musicians and politicians. President Jimmy Carter and his family once helicoptered here for lunch.

Dining at Seiryuso is a bounty of tasty and visual surprises—turquoise lacquer trays of pickled vegetables and *tamago yaki* ("sweet egg cake"), garnished with carrot cut in the shape of a gingko leaf and delicacies from the sea, served on fine bamboo branches. A famous local specialty is a deep-fried *okoze* fish, scorpion or rockfish, flavored with a fragrant lime-soy sauce.

Many of Seiryuso's 26 spacious rooms have garden or spa pool views. Twenty-four rooms have indoor private onsen baths. Complete with a spectacular pool, three communal *rotenburo*, a Roman-style sauna, a dry sauna and a vapor sauna, a banquet hall, a DVD theater and a library, Seiryuso is an oasis of luxury. Tall green bamboo gracefully sway. Torches light the night. The mineral waters are ever warm.

Address: 2-2 Kochi, Shimoda-shi, Shizuoka-ken 415-0011, Japan. **Tel:** 81 (0)558 22 1361. **Fax:** 81 (0)558 23 2066. **Website:** www.seiryuso.co.jp. **E-mail:** info@seiryuso.co.jp. **Rooms:** 26. **Access:** 2 hrs 30 min from Tokyo to Shimoda Station by Izu Express Line and 5 min to Seiryuso by taxi.

Senjyuan 仙寿庵   Minakami, Gunma

The noble strength of a mountain at your doorstep. The peaceful privilege of centering and easing into a natural spring bath drawn for you alone. Senjyuan's name lures: "Small Hermitage for a Long Life." This pavilion for longevity is a contemporary inn cherishing the simple lines, the clean spaces and elegance of a Sukiya-style house. Prize-winning architecture and a proprietary eye to preserving the very best of Japanese ryokan tradition set Senjyuan apart from other inns in the Tanigawa Onsen region.

Blonde rice stalks line the corridor to the dining rooms. Lighting is soft and frequently natural. Glass picture windows showcase the sweet pinks of cherry blossoms or muted grays and greens of stones and native grasses just beyond the mist of private hot spring water baths. Senjyuan leads a tiny generation of cosseting ryokan prepared to offer guests naturally sourced spring water in the privacy of their rooms. Spacious communal bathing with a view is also available.

Only two hours from Tokyo and 10 minutes from Minakami, the popular skiing and hiking area, Senjyuan is tucked at the foot of Tanigawa-dake, the mountain dividing Gunma Prefecture from Niigata Prefecture. Weather on the mountain is remarkably unpredictable. Sun one minute, snow the next makes for dramatic climbing and ever-changing views. A nearby cable car offers hikers a ride up to Tenjin-daira, where they can enjoy vistas of the Kanto Plain and the Sea of Japan.

Designed by world-renowned architect Takao Habuka, Senjyuan opened in 1997, the realization of the passion of owner Tomio Kubo, chairman of the Association for the Preservation of Japanese Ryokan. Mr Kubo also owns the more classic and rustic Ryokan Tanigawa, but it is with Senjyuan that he expands the definition of traditional Japanese hospitality. The delightful melding of traditional and contemporary

lines incorporated in Senjyuan garnered an architecture award in 1998. Its 18 rooms are all grand in scale; all offer guests the option of a solitary open-air soak. Based on the humble simplicity of tea cottages of the Muromachi Period (1333–1573), Senjyuan celebrates natural materials: plaster, bamboo, fragile Japanese paper, polished Japanese cypress.

Dinner and breakfast are not served in guest rooms, but in a variety of private dining rooms. The chef's artful temptations have already brought Senjyuan fame for serving one of the best ryokan cuisine in all of Japan. Creamy rice porridge, soft-boiled eggs, tangy pickled vegetables, breakfast here is traditional, presentation is heartwarmingly creative and attentive to detail.

Trees in the Tanigawa area astound with their autumn mosaic of color. The reds, siennas and golds of maple and beech trees make this a highly popular fall destination. Best to book six months in advance.

Address: Tanigawa-Nishidaira, Minakami-cho, Tone-gun, Gunma-ken 379-1619, Japan. **Tel:** 81 (0)278 20 4141. **Fax:** 81 (0)278 72 1860. **Website:** www.ryokan-tanigawa.com. **E-mail:** senjyuan@ryokan-tanigawa.com. **Rooms:** 18. **Access:** 1 hr 50 min drive from Nerima IC to Minakami IC by Kanetsu-Jidoshado and 5 min drive to Senjyuan, or 1 hr 20 min from Tokyo to Jyomo Kogen Station by Jyoetsu Shinkansen and 30 min to Senjyuan by taxi.

Bankyu Ryokan 本家伴久万久旅館 Yunishigawa, Tochigi

Step into a faraway forest, into a time of lords and warriors, of power struggles, banishment and retreat. The Ban family name is a name held with reverence and pride in remote Yunishigawa. The *honke*, or "main branch," of this highly esteemed family is a descendant of Taira no Kiyomori, a mighty ruler in the Heian Period (794–1185). Thanks to a humiliating battle in the 12th century, an entourage of Taira (also known as Heike) warrior families were driven from the Imperial court in Kyoto and set on a path that would lead them to the remote streams and springs and shielding woods of the naturally hot mineral waters found at Yunishigawa Onsen.

That long ago loss is today's secret to peace and architectural preservation. Bankyu Ryokan was built in 1666 and, not surprisingly, is one of the oldest ryokan in the area. Yunishigawa Village is within the 200,000 acres of Nikko National Park, a popular tourist destination, home to the Toshogu Shrine, the elaborate resting place of Ieyasu Tokugawa, Japan's most famous shogun, and to forests and mountains that have been considered sacred for more than 1,200 years.

Yunishigawa is itself an off-the-beaten-track destination partly because of its challenging accessibility. Yunishigawa is at least one-and-a-half hours' drive from more typical tourism sights. But it is the meticulously preserved traditions of a once fierce family that now call to curious souls from throughout Japan and around the world.

The present owner of Bankyu Ryokan, Teruhiko Ban, is of the 26th generation descended from the ancient Heike warriors. The grand-hostess of the ryokan is Tamae Ban, the owner's mother, and the noble woman behind the annual Great Heike Festival, Heike Ochiudo Taisai, which takes place in June. For every year in recent memory, Tamae Ban, primly bedecked in courtly silk kimono, has played the role of Tokiko, wife of Taira no Kiyomori in dramatic processions of samurai and court nobles.

When the weight of impassioned history overwhelms, some Bankyu guests can retreat to three rooms with private onsen baths overlooking the Yunishigawa River. Within the ryokan's confines there are also three outdoor onsen, one for men, one for women, a mixed bath and three additional private family-sized *rotenburo*. There are also four indoor onsen, two for ladies of the court, two for reflective warriors.

The ryokan is a big farmhouse of 45 rooms decorated with calligraphy, ikebana and the solid beams of camphor trees. Meals are taken in one big riverside dining room over individual open hearths (*irori*). River fish, deer, fowl and grilled meats are among the 15 dishes served as well as specialties that date from the Heike Period. Food is wild mountain fresh and simple, and guests are taught the subtleties of personally cooking over a charcoal hearth.

The festival in June is an unforgettable experience that keeps this ancient inn humming. Best to book three months in advance.

Address: 749 Yunishigawa, Kuriyama-mura, Shioya-gun, Tochigi-ken 321-2601, Japan. **Tel:** 81 (0)288 98 0011. **Fax:** 81 (0)288 98 0666. **Website:** www.bankyu.co.jp. **E-mail:** info@bankyu.co.jp. **Rooms:** 45. **Access:** 2 hrs from Tobu Asakusa to Yunishigawa Onsen Station by Tobu Aizu-kinugawa line and 30 min to Yunishigawa by bus.

Sanraku 山楽 Nasu, Tochigi

To contemplate a tree, a beech, perhaps a maple. "Magnificent Space," or Miyabi-no Ma, is the name of the second-floor room once visited by His Majesty, Showa Emperor Hirohito. He slept here, and it is said, was so moved by the painterly scenery of the fields of Nasu, stretching far and wide, that he was inspired to build an Imperial villa in Nasu.

The highlands of Nasu are within a two-hour drive north of Tokyo, so summers are peopled with vacationing families heading to the hills for mountain breezes, hiking trails and distractions from the intense urban heat. In fact, distractions abound: a Monkey Park, a Teddy Bear Museum, a Golf Garden and a Country Club, classic cars, antique jewelry, famous azaleas, an art museum dedicated to trees. Since the 1920s, Tochigi Prefecture's Nasu and Nagano Prefecture's Karuizawa have playfully rivaled as the preferred holiday home resorts for big-city dwellers.

Sanraku was opened over 80 years ago, but was elegantly remodeled in restrained tea-ceremony style in 1982. A tale is told of the nearby Nasu Onsen, "Deer Spring." Its healing waters were first discovered due to the misfortune of a wounded deer. Hunters came upon a hobbled deer, soothing its needy leg in the warm, mineral-rich waters. Sanraku's outdoor bathing offers peace of a primordial time. Fellow tourists are left behind; the natural refuge of the inn's onsen is only available to guests.

Garden views are everywhere. Pine trees and the abstract edges of hewn rock compete with Japanese painting and ceramics for guests' attention. At dinner, Sanraku displays and nourishes with myriad Japanese culinary specialties. Sashimi, sake, steamed rice and tofu, teppanyaki-grilled mushrooms, beef and sweet squash are beautifully served in frosted glass and tiny ceramic pieces of blue, pure white and marigold.

Summer here brings huge crowds. With the Mount Jeans Ski Resort conveniently nearby, Christmas and New Year's are also high season at Sanraku. To revel in the earthy crunch of autumn leaves beneath a boot, a running shoe, to smile at the sky through the veil of fiery red lace canopies of Japanese maples. Sanraku shelters a setting fit for an emperor or a humble aesthetic.

Address: 206 Yumoto, Nasu-machi, Nasu-gun, Tochigi-ken 325-0301, Japan. **Tel:** 81 (0)287 76 3010. **Fax:** 81 (0)287 76 4638. **Website:** www.e-sanraku.com. **E-mail:** sanraku@peach. ocn.ne.jp. **Rooms:** 38. **Access:** 1 hr 15 min from Tokyo to Nasu-Shiobara Station by Tohoku Shinkansen and 20 min to Sanraku by taxi, or 2 hrs drive from Nerima IC to Nasu IC by Tohoku-Jidosha-Do and 20 min drive to Sanraku on Route 17.

Hiiragiya 柊屋 Kyoto

Free our minds of the future. Hold dear the simple beauties of the past, the luxurious comforts of the present.

"Only at Hiiragiya does time stand still," wrote Nobel Prize-winning author Yasunari Kawabata, who repeatedly returned here to write in the classic, elegant rooms he equated with the many worlds of old Japan. First established in 1818, Hiiragiya ("House of the Holly Trees") has been owned and managed by the same family for six generations. Members of the Imperial family, scientists, politicians, artists and writers have made this small inn their temporary Kyoto home. Charlie Chaplin and Pierre Cardin slept here. The innkeeper's motto is prominently displayed in the entry: *Kuru mono, kaeru gotoshi*—that a guest at Hiiragiya might feel "as if he has come home."

Stones leading from the main gate to the front doorstep are splashed with water, which, in Japan, is a symbol of welcome. Guests are anticipated, and all is in order, awaiting their arrival. The wood has been polished, and the fresh flowers arranged just so.

Each of the 30 rooms has been distinctly decorated in harmonious Japanese style. The unaffected beauty of lustrous wood beams, delicate tatami mats, bamboo blinds and reed ceilings are the hallmarks of Hiiragiya. Paper doors and windows, sand and clay walls, polished wood frames, ceramic tiles and mats of straw are the architectural details that make up a typical room. Some of these rooms are over 100 years old. Twenty-six rooms have private bathrooms. Most rooms have views of the stone lantern, the bamboo fountain, the sculpted topiary bushes of the internal garden. There are three central baths that can be reserved for families or couples. One communal bath is decorated with stained glass, another with lacquer.

Dinner and breakfast are served in guests' rooms and feature the freshest of Kyoto seasonal cuisine, all graciously and beautifully presented. Sliced squid and salmon roe with a slice of lime, shrimp decorated with ferns and holly are served on Kiyomizu ceramics or fine lacquerware.

Hiiragiya is in an ideal Kyoto location, only 10 minutes from cherished Kyoto sites, such as Kiyomizudera and the geisha homes of Gion.

The inn is within walking distance of Nijo Castle, the old Imperial Palace and Honnoji Temple, and is not far from Heian Shrine. Here, there is a heightened attention to detail, a hushed, hallowed appreciation for the subtleties of nature and the importance of taking time to appreciate the changing of the seasons, flowers, birds, wind and moon.

Kawabata strolled here. He sipped green tea and captured a feeling of sublime contentment. He left us his words of invitation: "On a drizzly afternoon in Kyoto, sitting by the window, I watch the rain, listen to it fall…it is here that I wistfully recall the sense of tranquility that belonged to old Japan."

Address: Oike-kado, Fuya-cho, Nakakyo-ku, Kyoto 604-8094, Japan. **Tel:** 81 (0)75 221 1136. **Fax:** 81 (0)75 221 1139. **Website:** www.hiiragiya.co.jp. **E-mail:** info@hiiragiya.co.jp. **Rooms:** 30. **Access:** 2 hrs from Tokyo to Kyoto Station by Tokaido Shinkansen and 15 min to Hiiragiya by taxi.

Seikoro Inn 晴鴨樓　Kyoto

City life is revved up, immediate, tense, stimulating to the extreme. With hundreds or thousands or even millions of people coming together in one place, can a city anywhere in the world ever be considered a place for retreat and healing? Indeed! In Japan, that city is Kyoto. Gardens and temples and simpler ways have been saved. They are here to find, to treasure.

Known also as "House of the Wild Goose in Fine Weather," Seikoro Inn has been welcoming wayfarers since 1831. It is a bit of a stretch to imagine this highly peopled area, only minutes from Kyoto Station, as a refuge for migrating geese, but it is only a block east of the Kamo River. And people from all over the world have found Seikoro Inn and stopped for the night. It is cozy, intimate and comforting; especially to travelers overwhelmed by their inability to readily communicate. The friendly owner of Seikoro, Kentaro Shiroyama, speaks English and is happy to help guests find the many paths to quiet beauty available in Kyoto.

Ryoanji Temple was first designed during the Muromachi Period in the 15th century. The garden of stones is abstract Zen at its most confounding or illuminating depending on the viewers' mindset on a given day. An ordered arrangement of white gravel and 15 rocks is preserved as a challenging philosophical and aesthetic statement. The simplicity of color, design and form helps quiet busy urban minds. For the restless, there is a 1,000-year-old pond to circumnavigate.

Coming home to Seikoro feels like entering the historic home of a favorite Japanese auntie. There are architectural style elements from the Edo and Meiji Periods, hand-painted sliding doors, mother-of-pearl inlaid lacquer tables, and antiques from Europe as well as Japan. Some rooms open out to a remarkable inner garden, lush with ferns, trees in seasonal bloom, elegant lanterns and sculpture in stone. A few rooms date from 120 years ago. They are in great demand. Room No 10 and Room No 21 are the traditional Japanese rooms to request. All 22 rooms have private bathrooms. There are two humble *ofuro*, also known as communal stone baths, which are available to either male or female guests. Do note that these two baths are not fed by natural spring waters.

Dinner and breakfast are served in guests' rooms. Raw shrimp with a dab of wasabi on an edible *shiso* leaf might be one of the many courses served. Traditional, but also very keen to allow guests the flexibility of seeing as much of Kyoto as possible on a brief visit, the owner will accommodate those who wish to stay at the inn without the usually requisite 9–15-course, two-hour feast.

As compared to other inns of similar quality in Kyoto and Japan, Seikoro Inn is most reasonably priced, and its rooms, therefore, always seem to be booked. Do try to avoid staying in the annex, if possible. The nine rooms in the annex have been added only relatively recently and are therefore not redolent of the same history as the rest of the ryokan.

Seikoro Inn is a center of warm Japanese hospitality in a city that can still show the world a unique history of Zen masterworks, celebrating moss and rock, sky and water.

Address: Tonyamachi, Gojo Sagaru, Higashiyama-ku, Kyoto 605-0907, Japan. **Tel:** 81 (0)75 561 0771. **Fax:** 81 (0)75 541 5481. **Website:** www.seikoro.com. **E-mail:** yoyaku@seikoro.com. **Rooms:** 22. **Access:** 2 hrs 30 min from Tokyo to Kyoto Station by Tokaido Shinkansen and 10 min to Seikoro by taxi.

Kikusuiro 菊水楼 Nara

A seat of splendid tranquility. An inn for the priests who made it so. Kikusuiro is the oldest ryokan in Nara, a town founded in 710 AD as the first capital of Japan. Nara was then called Heijo-kyo ("Citadel of Peace"). It was a city of fervent Buddhism, of flourishing craftsmanship, literature and arts. During a brief 74 years, pagodas, temples and shrines were built as places for pilgrimage, for chanting, for the contemplation of suffering, the cycle of life, paths to enlightenment. By 784 the politically powerful moved on, but centuries later, Nara remains a city of spiritual sustenance, a city of architectural national treasures.

Kikusuiro, or "Water Chrysanthemum Tower," opened 230 years ago as a lodging house for Buddhist priests-in-training. Priests and scholars, faithful followers as well as everyday tourists have found the tile-roofed buildings, the quiet grounds and the richly decorated tatami rooms of Kikusuiro a place of rest, of prayer, of historic weight. The Japanese government has designated the inn a tangible cultural asset.

Kikusuiro is located in a corner of the 1,300-acre Nara Park. The inn is just across from the temple of Kofuku-ji, with its five-story pagoda and priceless wooden Bodhisattva, statues and sculpture dating from the 12th century. The Great Buddha, Daibutsu, of Todaiji Temple, and the oldest wooden structure in the world that houses it, are across the park. Over 1,000 deer roam the park's grounds. They are considered to be "divine messengers."

The lovingly preserved traditional elegance of Kikusuiro has attracted titans of the commercial world as well as the spiritual. Men and women of finance, politics, industry and academia have, through the years, stayed at esteemed Kikusuiro. They have come for its presence, its delicious *kaiseki* meals and its very special service. Kikuno, considered Nara's most exquisite geisha, is frequently asked to entertain at Kikusuiro.

There is a banquet room for big occasions and an adjacent restaurant, but guests usually prefer to receive their meals in the privacy of their rooms. Precious hors d'oeuvres of shrimp, pickled vegetables and edible chrysanthemums, and sweet and salty *ayu*, a river fish, may be served.

The 13 rooms meld antique refinements such as low lacquer tables, silk scrolls and vibrant kimono with the latest in high-tech televisions. Rooms do have private bathrooms, but bathing is usually done at the men's or women's communal *ofuro*.

To walk the wooden corridors of Kikusuiro. To behold a Buddha of bronze and gold. To rest, to reflect, to be inspired by spirits of long ago.

Address: 1130 Takabatake-cho, Nara-shi, Nara-ken 630-8301, Japan. **Tel:** 81 (0)742 23 2001. **Fax:** 81 (0)742 26 0025. **Rooms:** 13. **Access:** 1 hr flight from Haneda to Itami Airport by ANA or JAL, 1 hr by limousine bus to Kintetsu Nara Station and 5 min to Kikusuiro by taxi.

Ryugon 龍言 Minami-Uomuma, Niigata

A fabulous winged creature, a *ryu*, a dragon. Fierce and strong and noble. Dwellings of the men who offered their lives for a famous feudal lord. Ryugon is an enthralling realization of the life force of historic preservation.

At a time when all things new, modern and efficient were so prized that history was casually demolished, Toshio Utsugi saved a gatehouse, farmers' and samurais' homes dating from the 1800s and moved them to Minami-Uonuma, a quiet farm town in Japan's fabled snow country. In 1964, from northern Japan, he brought this puzzle of structures that today make a thriving ryokan. The main building is from Shiozawa, other rooms from Takayanagi, and outbuildings are from closer to home. The seven traditional ryokan buildings are from the Bunka-Bunsai Period (1804–1829) and are typical of the residences of samurai serving Lord Kenshin Uesugi of Echigo, the historic name for Niigata.

Niigata Prefecture and especially Minami-Uonuma are favored destinations for travelers from throughout Japan. Crystal blue skies, bountiful snows, and the world-famous, highly treasured *nishiki-goi*, a particularly vibrant carp—not to mention the home paddies for Japan's most popular Koshihikari rice—have put Minami-Uonuma on many peoples' maps. The combination of flavorful rice and waters drawn from snow-rich mountains helped produce prized sake labels: Hakkaizan and Fuyu-Shogun. So, travelers come to ski, eat and drink, and yet another enticement awaits, as an oil company digging for natural gas in 1957 discovered by accident—hot natural spring waters!

At Ryugon there is hot waterfall bathing in waters rich with sodium chloride. There are two indoor communal onsen, two outdoor communal *rotenburo* and an additional two garden *rotenburo* that can each accommodate as many as 40

bathers. Two family-sized *rotenburo* can be reserved for 40 minutes at a time for an additional fee. Guests are welcome to take to the waters all night and all day.

Most of the inn's rooms are built in *chumon-zukuri* design, a style that was typical for residences of high-ranking samurai. Long wooden corridors connect the rooms. Nearly all of the rooms have garden views of ponds and snowy or verdant mountain peaks. The rooms are simply but distinctly decorated with calligraphy scrolls, intricately carved wood transoms and artfully designed *shoji* doors. There are rooms for conferences, pottery and painting, a restaurant and pub, and a karaoke house. Meals are usually served in guests' rooms. The *kaiseki* parade of intriguing flavors might feature egg cake, salt roasted *ayu*—the popular freshwater fish—a soothing bowl of miso with vegetables and of course, Koshihikari rice.

Ryugon is less than two hours from Tokyo via Shinkansen and local train, and only a 30-minute drive from skiing. It is a place of refreshing, tingling pure mountain air, thrilling and invigorating vertical trails of snowy white and evergreen, and warm sake, a hot mineral-rich bath, a cozy futon in a space of museum-caliber craft and construction.

Address: 79 Sakado, Minami-Uonuma-shi, Niigata-ken 949-6611, Japan. **Tel:** 81 (0)25 772 3470. **Fax:** 81 (0)25 772 2124. **Website:** www.ryugon.co.jp. **E-mail:** info@ryugon.co.jp. **Rooms:** 32. **Access:** 1 hr 20 min from Ueno to Echigo-Yuzawa Station by Jyoetsu-Shinkansen and 20 min to Ryugon by taxi, or 2 hrs 45 min drive from Nerima IC in Tokyo to Minami-Uonuma IC by Kanetsu Jidoshado and 10 min drive to Ryugon.

Yumoto Choza 湯元長座 Kamitakara-mura

Mountain majesty. Peaks call to climbers. Summits are to be conquered or to be revered. Yumoto Choza is at the foot of the northern Japanese Alps.

It is very, very quiet here. There is no karaoke. There is birdsong of jay and bush warbler. There is no video arcade, no shopping mall. There is hiking and climbing and ambling and strolling. There is no pachinko parlor. There is fishing in the river for char or trout, or soaking in a soothing hot water bath. There is no movie theater. There are seasonally changing sceneries: snow-white pines, cherry pink blossoms, summer greens and blues, autumn reds and gingko yellows. There are white birch forests to wander, humble villages to explore, farmers' markets to meander and study and taste. Historic Matsumoto Castle is only one hour away.

It is for all that there is and isn't here that people come. With these extreme peaks, this extreme quiet, this feeling of old Japan and a remarkably reasonable price, Yumoto Choza is considered one of the 10 most popular ryokan in all of Japan. Wintertime is precious here. Book early and bring yen. No credit cards are accepted and little English is spoken.

Owner Takeo Kose likes to say that he offers a "traditional Japanese life and culture." In 1969 he built his inn of beams and boards saved and assembled from an old Niigata home, local farmhouses and sake breweries. There is no fluorescent lighting, but there are atmospheric paper lanterns and the glow of *irori* ("sunken hearths"). Eighteen of the 32 rooms have private *irori*. In two special rooms, guests can grill mountain vegetables, mushrooms, beef or mutton and potatoes over an open hearth. There might be skewers of chewy miso-flavored rice cakes, *ayu*, the small white fish, or vegetarian tempura. There will most probably be creamy tofu served in a small sea of soy sauce.

Only two rooms have private bathrooms, but there are two large indoor baths of *hinoki*—a type of Japanese cypress—and two *rotenburo*. Down by the Hirayu River there are another two men's and women's open-air baths, and the inn also has three family-sized baths.

It takes two-and-a-half hours by express train to reach Matsumoto Station, then another hour to drive to this unaffected alpinist's base camp. The journey itself from whirring city to sedate village is almost welcome. The transition could be rather startling. Left behind are extravagances of this modern age. Yumoto Choza cherishes extravagances of a simpler time: pure mountain air, fertile, fragrant earth, magical warming fire, waters of delightful taste and touch.

Address: Fukuchi Onsen, Kamitakara-mura, Kichijyou-gun, Gifu-ken 506-1434, Japan. **Tel:** 81 (0)578 9 0099. **Fax:** 81 (0)578 9 2010. **Rooms:** 32. **Access:** 2 hrs 30 min from Tokyo to Matsumoto Station by Express Train Azusa and 1 hr to Fukuchi Onsen by taxi or bus.

Wanosato 倭乃里 Miya-mura, Gifu

Abundant trees in all their stalwart magnificence. Their timber strength and the Hida area's highly skilled craftsmen were once the only currency villages could offer a taxing shogun. Taxes in the eighth century were paid in grains of rice, but this region was not agriculturally rich enough to send an adequate amount of rice. Instead, it sent timber and carpenters to Nara, Kyoto and Edo to build temples, shrines and courts.

Wanosato, or "Japanese Country Village," is 20 minutes' drive south of Takayama, nestled in the snowy mountains of the Japan Alps in northern Gifu. Due to its remote location, (a five-hour journey from Tokyo by Shinkansen and local train) Takayama and the nearby Hida Folk Village have been able to preserve an admirable collection of sake breweries, merchant houses and shops dating from the Edo Period (1615–1868).

Wanosato is itself a charming collection of lovingly restored 100- to 150-year-old farmhouses carefully transplanted in 1990 from Kamioka, Gifu, comprising four independent villas and a main building with another four rooms overlooking the Miya River and a lush garden of forest green. Like fairytale cottages, several buildings have roofs thatched with two- to three-foot thick miscanthus, a type of pampas grass.

These old-world houses are often called *gassho-zukuri* houses, and are so named for their particularly steep-sloped roofs—*gassho* translates as "praying hands." While most roofs in Japan are at angles of 45 degrees, *gassho* roofs slope at around 60 degrees so that snow and rain will quickly run off and the grass roofs can rapidly dry. These houses are marvels of ingenious design. No nails are used in the roofs. Straw rope binds timber and roof braces. Slats in the ceiling allow for natural ventilation. Smoke from central interior hearths rises into the rafters, helps dry the pampas and discourage insects. With the proper frequency of smoke, one of these picturesque roofs can last as long as 50 years.

Hearth smoke wafts through the lobby of Wanosato's main building. In the evening, sake is warmed in canes of bamboo briefly set among the hot ash. Breakfast and dinner are served in guests' rooms or in a dining room in one of the main buildings. Each dish is presented on a distinct piece of Japanese ceramics, blue and white porcelain or rough, earthy clay. The array of soup and tofu and vegetables and fish and rice and fruit is selected to honor all that is of the season.

From the two grand indoor wooden onsen the picture-window views are seasonal celebrations of maple and beech. All eight rooms have private bathrooms. Both indoor hot springs are sourced in the main building.

Wanosato is a Japanese village scene from long ago. Carp swim. A waterwheel turns. Light and shadows play off polished cypress floors. Grand-hostess Kabeya-san makes all who enter feel welcome with her smile. Little English is comprehended.

The spring and autumn festivals in Takayama are considered among the best in all of Japan. Mighty timbers shout with ostentatious leafy brilliance in April and October. Wise seekers of forest tranquility reserve a year in advance.

Address: 1682 Miya-mura, Ohno-gun, Gifu-ken, 509-3538, Japan. Tel: 81 (0)577 53 2321. Fax: 81 (0)577 53 3220. Rooms: 8. Access: 2 hrs from Tokyo to Nagoya Station by Tokaido Shinkansen, 2 hrs 30 min to Takayama Station by local train and 20 min to Wanosato by taxi.

Kayotei かよう亭 Yamanaka, Ishikawa

"Seat of ennoblement," Sukiya style at its most understated elegance, its most discreetly exquisite and uncommon. Here at Kayotei, there are intimate spaces influenced by the West and nature known for inspiring the pearls of a haiku poet.

Kaga and Yamanaka Onsen are far west of Tokyo and nearly on the Sea of Japan. The Buddhist priest Gyoki first discovered Yamanaka's hot spring waters over a thousand years ago. In the 1970s, Masanori Kamiguchi inherited a vast Yamanaka ryokan, but big was not the statement Mr Kamiguchi wished to make. In 1978, after years of consideration and study with an architect, craftsman and a chef, Mr Kamiguchi opened intimate, sublime Kayotei Inn. His mission has been to provide a "seat" for the very best of local art and culture.

Designed in the Sukiya style of a tea cottage from the Muromachi Period (1333–1573), and graced with very subtle decorative touches, The Kayotei Inn mixes antique *tansu* chests of drawers, low polished oak tables, hand-painted screens, traditional ceramic pieces and modern sculptural designs. There are a mere 10 Japanese-style rooms, six of which have private bathrooms. There are two indoor communal mineral water baths splendidly walled in spans of glass, providing guests with onsen views of maple forest sceneries.

The Kayotei Inn is set at the beginning of a lovely walking trail following the perimeter of Kakusen Gorge, about a half-hour south of Kanazawa. Along the path is a thatched arbor dedicated to Haiku poet Basho Matsuo, who wrote of these trees and skies and waters in the 1600s.

During a period of much instability in Japan, the Kanazawa area, then known as Kaga, was the stronghold of the Maeda lords, who brought peace and riches to these lands. While the rest of Japan rushed to modernize, Kanazawa centered on its arts

and still today is a city rich with culture. The Kenroku-en Garden is considered one of Japan's best. There are centuries-old shops selling handcrafted *shamisen*, gold-leaf and kimono silks. Yamanaka *nuri* ("lacquerware") is highly regarded in Japan.

Meals are taken in the privacy of guests' rooms. English is well understood, and Kayotei's hosts are keen to please. Attentive service is of such importance at The Kayotei Inn that it is not unusual for the inn's owner or general manager to personally guide guests to the lacquer and ceramics workshops of Yamanaka. Right under Kayotei's roof is a culinary artisan whose creativity, dexterity and passion for fresh and rare ingredients is helping to promote this Japanese spa inn as a gourmand's destination. For dinner, Chef Susumu Ishimasa, author of *The Dishes of Kayotei*, might serve a soup of quail, shrimp and snow peas in the cool freshness of a winter gourd, artistically presented on a garden-green vine, and sashimi of white fish and squid on a blanket of crushed ice, shredded *daikon*, soy sauce and wasabi as accompaniments. But, it is the breakfast at The Kayotei Inn that brings seasoned guests back. Creamy tofu, grilled fish and precious cubes of sweet buttery egg come together as a most memorable Japanese beginning to the day.

Address: Higashi-machi, Yamanaka-cho, Enuma-gun, Ishikawa-ken 922-0114, Japan. **Tel:** 81 (0)761 78 1410. **Fax:** 81 (0)761 78 1121. **Rooms:** 10. **Access:** 1 hr flight from Haneda to Komatsu Airport and 30 min to Yamanaka by taxi.

Araya Totoan あらや滔々庵   Yamashiro, Kaga

The sparkle of snow on cedar. The chilling thrill of stepping across a footbridge to sip sake in a villa that once served as a weekend retreat for a member of the Imperial family. One must slightly bow beneath a fabric *noren* curtain to enter the long corridor gently lit with paper lanterns. This corridor leads to the wooden bridge above a flowing brook. Arisugawa-Sanso, the former Imperial families' house in the woods, is, in its present incarnation, a candlelit bar with several intimate nooks for conversation as well as the telling of tales.

It was Genemon Araya, who first established Araya Totoan. He was keeper of the keys, the caretaker of the thermal waters of Yamashiro for the Lord Maeda clan in the mid-1600s. The present owner of Araya Totoan, Takayuki Nagai, is an 18th-generation Araya. It is easy to understand why the waters here in the Kaga area of Ishikawa Prefecture were once the favorite of nobility. These thermal waters are remarkable for their soft touch and their soothing nature. Onsen *tamago*, eggs boiled in these waters, are considered a treasured delicacy and, as such, are a treat sold in the food halls of Takashimaya in Tokyo.

The spa bathing at Araya Totoan is unforgettable. There are two communal hot spring baths in nature and two communal indoor onsen. All of the 20 rooms at Araya Totoan have private bathrooms and five rooms have delightful private hot spring baths. With its Kaga red walls, so colored to honor the local lord, its Sukiya design using sliding paper doors, cushioned tatami space and slivers of alcove for a single blossom, a silk scroll, the Ochin-no-Ma room is exemplary of the refined living spaces at Araya Totoan.

The iconoclastic potter and gourmet Rosanjin Kitaoji was so fond of this area that in the 1930s he charmed his way into the hearts of local ryokan owners as he studied the making of colorful *kutani-yaki* under the famous potter Seika Suda. The Kaga Onsen area, which includes Yamashiro Onsen as well as Yamanaka Onsen and Awazu Onsen, is renowned throughout Japan for its production of *kutani-yaki*. In the 17th century *kutani-yaki* was first exported to Europe. Seika Suda had his own kiln in Yamashiro and produced numerous masterpieces here.

It was here too that Rosanjin, as he was familiarly known, experimented with clay and concepts for serving delicious dishes. His Tokyo restaurant, Hoshigaoka-Saryo, was world-famous in the 1930s for serving Japanese delicacies on one-of-a-kind plates and vessels of art. Today some of Rosanjin's pots are shown at Rosanjin's former home, Iroha-Souan, in Yamashiro. The artistry of Rosanjin can also be seen in the lobby of Araya Totoan. In exchange for the support of his accommodating innkeepers, Rosanjin presented his handmade wares. The 17th owner of Araya Totoan, Shunjiro Nagai, was also the mayor of Yamashiro. In appreciation of his support, Rosanjin carved the inn's nameboard and left gifts of calligraphy and pottery.

The novel presentation of delicacies at Araya Totoan is worthy of this gourmet artisan. Wintertime crab is served on leaves of bamboo, and roasted white fish, slightly salted *edamame*, thin pink ginger roots and pickled radish, on plates of *kutani-yaki*, or platters of lacquer. If in season, persimmons make an appearance on the menu as autumnal orange cups filled with seafood, sweet sticky gingko nuts and mountain potatoes. There is always warm sake and hot waters worthy of lords and itinerant potters.

Address: Yamashiro Onsen, Kaga-shi, Ishikawa-ken 922-0242, Japan. **Tel:** 81 (0)761 77 0010. **Fax:** 81 (0)761 77 0008. **Website:** www.araya-totoan.com. **E-mail:** info@araya-totoan.com. **Rooms:** 20. **Access:** 1 hr flight from Haneda to Komatsu Airport and 30 min to Yamashiro by taxi.

Houshi 法師 Awazu Onsen, Komatsu

A venerable sanctuary for healing. A wooden inn of esteemed age and contemplative hospitality. In 718 AD, the Buddhist priest Garyo Houshi was ordered by a ministering elder to build a therapeutic retreat near the mineral springs of Awazu. He was to provide a setting of wellness for the many who suffered from diseases of the day.

The waters of Awazu, south of Komatsu in Ishikawa Prefecture, continue to provide comfort more than 1,300 years later. And Houshi, 46 generations later and now under the stewardship of Zengoro Houshi, still welcomes with warmth and compassion. Upon arrival, guests are greeted with the meditative presentations, the turns and the gentleness of the tea ceremony. The bowl is a work of art. The foam of green tea is stunning. Its strong, scented warmth is revitalizing.

Houshi has been listed as the "oldest wooden hotel in the world" in the *Guinness Book of World Records*. It is the oldest and one of only two Japanese members of les Henokiens, an association of multi-generational family enterprises whose members can all tout at least 200-year-old ancestry.

Tea in the spacious entry tatami room opens to a view of the moss garden that is said to have been designed by tea master and garden designer Enshu Kobori— the same architect of stones and green who created many of Kyoto's temple and castle gardens—sometime in the 1600s. All of Houshi's 74 rooms overlook the antique trees that in winter are protected from heavy snows by sculptural shields and swathes of bamboo. All rooms have private bathrooms, floors of fragrant reed tatami, low wooden tables set for tea, ikebana flowers in the *tokonoma* alcove, crisp cotton *yukata*, white *tabi* socks and towels ready for onsen bathing. There are two indoor spa baths, two open-air *rotenburo* and one *kazoku-buro*, or "family bath."

Dinner and breakfast, served in the intimacy of guests' rooms, are prepared with great tea master Sen-no-Rikyu's considerate *bons mots* in mind: make guests feel cool in summer, warm in winter. The freshest fish from the nearby Sea of Japan, succulent crab or shrimp or clams, may be served for dinner. There might be a porcelain cup of seaweed-cloaked tofu in warm soy sauce. In a sunflower-yellow china bowl there could be cod, mushrooms and lily root.

Throughout the ages the Houshi family has humbly received many noteworthy citizens, such as Prime Minister Taro Katsura during the Meiji Period (1868–1912). There is a special garden villa reserved for guests requiring such exclusive privacy. Its walls are painted in lordly Kaga red and blue. Its tatami is covered with a Persian carpet. Its name speaks of generations of nurturers of health and well-being. In this moss garden there is a shelter called Enmeikaku, or "Pavilion for a Long Life."

Address: Awazu Onsen, Komatsu-shi, Ishikawa-ken 923-0326, Japan. **Tel:** 81 (0)761 65 1111. **Fax:** 81 (0)761 65 1115. **Website:** www.ho-shi.co.jp. **E-mail:** ho-shi@ho-shi.co.jp. **Rooms:** 74. **Access:** 1 hr flight from Haneda to Komatsu Airport and 15 min to Awazu Onsen by taxi.

Mukaitaki 向瀧　Higashiyama, Aizu-Wakamatsu

To sleep, perhaps to dream among blossoms of azalea or cherry pink. These verdant trees are awash in fiesta colors in March and April and May. The Nadeshiko Room, named for yet another pretty pink flower, has a humbling view of a glorious cherry tree. Views from the Momiji ("Maple") Room make guests feel like their futon are floating among the trees.

The spas of Mukaitaki—"Facing a Waterfall"—are sourced from Higashiyama Onsen, which, it is said, were first discovered in the 740s by Gyoki, a Buddhist priest and spiritual leader who put many of Japan's hot springs on the map.

Mukaitaki was built in 1873 and was dubbed Fox Spa for the clever animal first found healing itself there. Aizu clansmen made this their health retreat for recovering from battle wounds. Former Japanese Prime Minister Tanaka Kakuei considered Mukaitaki one of his favorite ryokan.

Two-and-a-half hours from Tokyo by Shinkansen and express train, Mukaitaki is only 10 minutes from Tsuruga Castle in Aizu-Wakamatsu. "Castle of the Crane" is a reconstruction of the original fortress built by the Ashina clan in 1384. Today the interior of the castle houses a museum displaying Buddhist statues, ceramics and crafts produced in the area as well as Aizu *nuri*, the local lacquerware that has been internationally exported since 1717. From the fifth-story tower of the castle, there is an impressive view of the entire Aizu valley.

The gardens of Mukaitaki lie in that bucolic valley. Owned and managed by the Hirata family since 1873, Mukaitaki has been so lovingly preserved and updated that its wooden buildings are listed on the national registry.

The carving of wooden transom, the hand-painted sliding doors and latticed *shoji*-papered windows bear witness to generations of skilled craftsmen. Dinner is

served on Aizu's famous lacquerware. Carp stewed in sweet soy sauce, herring, and even horsemeat, are usually part of the feast. The dining room overlooks the interior garden, romantically illuminated at night.

The waters of Higashiyama Onsen contain sodium hydrosulfide, chloride and hypo-tonic alkaline, said to naturally benefit rheumatism, stomach and skin disease and arterial sclerosis. The elegant marble baths of the men's Monkey Spa feature a relief of a graceful bather. The hot, 110-degree-Fahrenheit waters sooth muscles and soften skin. Four small private baths, *kazokuburo*, are also available.

Flamboyant pink dreams are many when the azaleas are in bloom in May.

Address: Higashiyama-cho, Aizu-Wakamatsu-shi, Fukushima-ken 965-0814, Japan. **Tel:** 81 (0)242 27 7501. **Fax:** 81 (0)242 28 0939. **Website:** www.mukaitaki.com. **E-mail:** ryokan@mukaitaki.com. **Rooms:** 24. **Access:** 2 hrs 30 min from Tokyo to Aizu-Wakamatsu Station via Kooriyama by Tohoku Shinkansen and Banetsu-Saisen and 15 min to Higashiyama Onsen by taxi.

Saryo Soen 茶寮宗園 Akiu, Sendai

A tree, its leaves, mysteries of the mist, they teach us the marvels of nature. The slow turn of a tea bowl, the gentle whisking of warm water, these methodic rituals for the making of tea teach us to see. Saryo Soen is a "garden teahouse" on six-and-a-half acres of land, the boutique ryokan dream of owner, Shuichi Yamao, who hails from the same family that for over 10 generations has provided guests lodging at the esteemed 171-room Mitoya ryokan, Hotel New Mitoya, which is also located in the Akiu Onsen region.

Tearooms of the 16th century were the golf courses or the latte living rooms of today. Dealmakers came to match-make, samurai came to build alliances, contemplate victory or defeat. Opened in 1991, no expense has been spared at Saryo Soen to make this exclusive ryokan one of the top onsen ryokan in all of Japan. The guest list often includes international diplomats and Japanese CEOs, pleased to share their wisdom of the merits of Japanese tea, their acumen in selecting the finest of sake. Malaysian Prime Minister Mahathir slept here.

There are 26 rooms in all, one even offering a Western bed. Ten of the rooms are not housed within the two-story main building. They have their own private *rotenburo* as well as indoor baths. There are two communal baths, one for men, one for women. All rooms have their own individual details to appreciate. The tea-ceremony architecture is built of butter-hued Japanese cypress and masterfully makes use of glass picture windows to welcome natural lighting and incorporate the backdrop of nature with the most precious of inn artwork.

Freshly split bamboo chopsticks, skillfully sculpted vessels of lime rind and impromptu displays of autumn leaves reflect a focus on detail and presentation that is matched by the savory flavors of the inn's dinners and breakfasts. Meals here are to be tasted as well as seen.

Sendai, northern Japan's largest city, is less than two hours by Shinkansen from Tokyo. The Akiu Hot Springs along the Natori River are about a 40-minute drive west of town. Local legend has it that these springs cured an ill emperor more than 1,500 years ago. Its therapeutic salt waters are believed to help arthritis and lower-back pain. Matsushima, a bay with one of Japan's "three most famous views," is only an hour away. In the heart of the city is Zuiganji Temple, a Zen temple, over 900 years old and considered an architectural national treasure.

One of the most popular times of the year to visit Sendai is August 6–8 for the Tanabata Festival, which dates back to Heian Period (794–1185), and celebrates the one time in the year when the Weaver and the Herdsman, the stars Vega and Altair, are reunited by a bridge of magpies spreading over the Milky Way. Merry-makers write their innermost desires on colorful paper streamers, hang these from branches of bamboo and set them afloat along rivers or rice paddies to send away bad spirits.

It is advised to reserve more than three months in advance—this exquisite garden teahouse in Sendai draws guests from around the world.

Address: Akiu-cho, Taihaku-ku, Sendai-shi, Miyagi-ken 982-0241, Japan. **Tel:** 81 (0)22 398 2311. **Fax:** 81 (0)22 398 2144. **Rooms:** 26. **Access:** 1 hr 40 min from Tokyo to Sendai Station by Tohoku Shinkansen and 40 min to Saryo Soen by taxi.

Tsuru-no-Yu 鶴の湯 Tazawako, Akita

The hidden waters have been found. The secret is out.

It is said a crane (*tsuru*) first led hunters to this "hidden" hot spring. Today, it is necessary to book a room at this inn a full year in advance. Tsuru-no-Yu is one of the most popular "secret" onsen in all of Japan, and its appeal is not merely a matter of warm water.

The spirit of this retreat is so refreshingly authentic that trekkers and tourists and bathers alike are charmed by its persistence in leaving nature alone. Red chili peppers, rice stalks and fragrant persimmons hang to dry, flaunting a second beauty, a sense of sustainability learned long ago. The thatched-roof long house is over 100 years old, and with a little advance warning, guests can stew their mountain vegetables in miso over a sunken hearth.

Akita is a one-hour flight northeast of Tokyo and is famous as a rice-growing region. During the autumn harvest, the rice fields of Akita shine in gold. Nyuto Onsen and Tsuru-no-Yu are about a two-hour bus or car ride from Akita Airport. The trails and wildflowers of nearby Mount Komagatake are attractive to hikers, and history buffs are pleased to see that Kakunodate still has some well-preserved samurai houses.

The milky sulfur-rich waters of Nyuto Onsen are popular with these daytrippers, eager to toss off boots and cameras and steal moments soaking in nature's soothing aquatic gift. Tsuru-no-Yu shares this outdoor onsen with the public and graciously welcomes daytime bathers as well as paying inn guests. This open bath means less private privilege for guests, but Tsuru-no-Yu tastefully accommodates and pleases everyone by offering yummy lunch and tea fare at an unpretentious onsen site café. This big public pool is open to a mix of men and women, quite rare these days. At the inn, there are an additional three baths, two for women, one for men.

Elements of the Edo Period (1615–1868) remain alive here. Three hundred and fifty years ago, the *daimyo* of Kakunodate knew the "secret," and was such a regular he had his own pavilion. Thirteen consecutive generations dating from the Edo Period owned Tsuru-no-Yu until 1981, when Kazushi Sato purchased the fairytale house in the woods. Thanks to Mr Sato's determination to preserve the humble, solid beams of the past, Tsuru-no-Yu remains a cherished destination in part for its allure as a place that seems to have left time behind. Oil lamps light the night. The fee for lodging is remarkably reasonable. In spite of this inn's very simple and rustic nature, a room in mid-October must be cadged at least 12 months in anticipation. It is often difficult to find a room in the *honkan* ("main wing"). Annex rooms are to be avoided. They just aren't the same.

Autumn backdrops of lemony-leaved beeches and silvery pampas grass—behold.

Address: Tazawako-machi, Senboku-gun, Akita-ken 014-1204, Japan. **Tel:** 81 (0)187 46 2139. **Fax:** 81 (0)187 46 2761. **Website:** www.tsurunoyu.com. **Rooms:** 35. **Access:** 1 hr flight from Haneda to Akita Airport and 2 hrs drive to Nyuto Onsen by taxi or limousine bus, or 3 hrs from Tokyo to Tazawako by Akita Shinkansen and 30 min to Nyuto Onsen by taxi.

Kuramure 蔵群 Otaru, Hokkaido

Hmm. The nature of beauty. What is it? What is art? To get to this gallery-like ryokan one must go to the north, to Japan's land of fewest people, Hokkaido. The open landscapes of as many as six national parks stir the imaginations of skiers, bicyclists and hikers, and have also inspired watercolorists, Haiku poets and impassioned novelists.

It is a one-and-a-half hour flight from Tokyo's Haneda Airport to Kuramure's closest airport, Chitose, south of Sapporo, then another hour by train to the town of Otaru. Kuramure is in Asarigawa Onsen on a hillside about 10 minutes' car ride from Otaru Station. Yes, it is remote, but, ah, what a happy surprise awaits those who make the journey!

Kuramure means "group of warehouses," and warehouses represent the bustling history of Otaru. Since the 17th century, merchant vessels with fish and timber, rice and silks, porcelain and oranges have been entering and exiting this port town on the Sea of Japan. The waters off the coast have supplied such wealthy stores of herring that fishermen were able to build grand *nishin-goten* ("herring castles"), luxurious homes that fascinate tourists even today.

Prize-winning architect Makoto Nakayama found beauty in the fortitude of Otaru's storehouses, and in 2002, with owner Toshiyuki Sanada, built a new-age warehouse for contemporary art and design, healing, bathing, refined dining and fun. Orbs and eggs, patterns and textures, planes of wood and water represent art and beauty, but so do Le Corbusier chairs, contemporary sculpture by local artists and Asian antiques. The dramatic power of a cage of rock contrasts with the polished wood of a simple colonial bench. Art might be a stone lantern, a graceful tree, an ordered arrangement of white pebbles. Ceramic vases for ikebana floral sculptures represent art of a different kind.

Kuramure has four natural springs available to guests, two communal outdoor baths, two indoor, one for men and one for women. There are 15 semi-Western-style rooms with beds, and four traditional Japanese-style rooms. Rooms are named for novelists, poets and painters who at some point had an affiliation with Otaru. Dinner and breakfast are served in a separate dining room. The *kaiseki* fare features shrimp and crab and locally grown herbs and vegetables. There are elements of Italian, French and Chinese cuisine in the numerous dishes served.

Owner Sanada's fresh approach to Japanese inn-keeping can be sensed every-where. The emphasis on using materials of the earth, stone, iron, mud and handmade Japanese paper, is sophisticated and welcome. Making guests comfortable and at ease is a priority. The bar is staffed with friendly young students, some of whom are from Europe and the Americas. English is readily understood here.

Andy Warhol's Factory in the 1960s was a warehouse salon for exaggerated experiments in the meaning of art. In Hokkaido, there is also a salon warehouse with natural waters and playful juxtapositions of art in many forms.

Address: 2-685 Asarigawa Onsen, Otaru-shi, Hokkaido 047-0154, Japan. Tel: 81 (0)134 51 5151. Fax: 81 (0)134 51 5000. Website: www.kuramure.com. E-mail: international@ kuramure.com. Rooms: 19. Access: 1 hr 30 min flight from Haneda to Chitose Airport, 1 hr to Otaru-Chikuko by JR train and 5 min to Kuramure by taxi.

Sekitei 石亭   Ohno-cho, Hiroshima

So mesmerizing the sea. Its rhythms calm, its crashing waves energize. On a hillside overlooking the Inland Sea, Sekitei is a garden of peace, not far from a city that bravely stands as a testament to the humbling importance of peace, *heiwa*, freedom from wars.

Sekitei is 30 minutes from Hiroshima Airport or 15 minutes from Miyajimaguchi Pier Terminal. To face the setting of such inhumane destruction is a pilgrimage many feel they must make. Hiroshima's tales are haunting and now inspiring. Sekitei's lawns of green, gentle warm spring waters and vista of the holy island of Miyajima help to ease pains past and present.

Miyajima is a sacred site of both Buddhism and Shintoism and is considered one of Japan's most beautiful views. The vermilion shrine gate (*torii*) seemingly afloat in the sea, is a fascinating image of a noble entrance keeper to a precious place. Itsukushima Shrine on Miyajima was first constructed in 593 AD. Japan has officially listed it as an extraordinary example of sacred architecture and a national treasure.

Across the water, Sekitei ryokan has a quiet beauty and 10 Japanese-style rooms for the night. Seven rooms have private bathrooms.

Sekitei was built in 1965 and is managed by Jyunichi Ueno, whose clever ancestor in 1901 concocted a savory dish that remains a local pride. *Anago-meshi*, a rice bowl topped with sea eel baked in sweet soy sauce, is the special lunch of choice for tourists visiting Miyajima. Of course, the original recipe served at Sekitei is incomparable and many stop for the privilege of merely dining at Sekitei. Wafer-thin sliced raw *fugu*, blowfish, oysters, sea urchin and locally harvested vegetables are also served in one-of-a-kind ceramic pieces. The inn offers guests the choice of simpler fare or rarest of delicacies. Ryokan guests are served dinner and breakfast

in the privacy of their rooms, but there is also a banquet room that can accommodate parties of 50. Tea or coffee might be served in the garden overlooking the water.

There are five communal hot springs, two indoor, one each for men and women,
and three outdoor. There are waves of Zen raked stones, expansive green grass, and
walls of latticed paper that slide to alter views by minute, by night, by day. Sculptural
paper lanterns light the dark of night. Bathe in a warm tub of Japanese cypress in a
place that speaks only of peace.

Address: Miyahama Onsen, Ohno-cho, Saeki-gun, Hiroshima-ken 739-0454, Japan.
Tel: 81 (0)829 55 0601. **Fax:** 81 (0)829 55 0603. **Website:** www.sekitei.to. **E-mail:**
info@sekitei.to. **Rooms:** 10. **Access:** 1 hr 30 min flight from Haneda to Hiroshima Airport
and 30 min to Miyahama by taxi.

Yamatoya Besso 大和屋別荘 Dogo, Matsuyama

Writers of impassioned phrasing were here inspired. Hot spring waters, a feudal castle keep and turrets, camellias and mandarin oranges have attracted scholars and poets and at least one novelist of note.

On Shikoku Island in Matsuyama, the city of one of Japan's finer remaining castles, circa 1603, there is a mineral water source that is said to be one of the oldest in Japan. Dogo Onsen Honkan dates from 1894. From its interior, the bath building looks very much like a small wooden castle. The ceiling of the *honkan*, or main building, is graced with a legendary white heron. A large bell is rung at 6:30 every morning to announce the opening of the bath. Dogo Onsen Honkan has such a hallowed atmosphere that guests staying at neighboring ryokan with their own private mineral water sources still wish to soak in the more public and often crowded Honkan baths.

Yamatoya Besso is only a two- to three-minute walk from Dogo Onsen Honkan and offers modern-day luxuries with its own history and hot soothing waters. This "second home" was originally built in 1868, but was closed and totally rebuilt in the 1980s. The owners, the Okumura family, traveled throughout Japan and studied the country's most refined inns. Today's Yamatoya Besso is light and spacious, a highly tasteful melding of elegant Sukiya understatement with more modern comforts.

The inn's natural cypress interiors are artfully lit and judiciously accented with gold-leaf screens, small silk-clad dolls and intriguing haiku scrolls. The 17 syllables of locally well-known poets are dramatically on display in a gallery of haiku. Guests are often encouraged to find quiet moments for reflection and their own wordplay.

Writer Soseki Natsume (1867–1916), whose face is printed on the 1,000-yen note, was assigned to teach English at the Ehime Prefectural Middle School in

1895. His impressions of the area have been immortalized in his well-known novel, *Botchan*. At Dogo Onsen Honkan there is a room with photos of the man who first imagined the memorable character Botchan. Today there is a little "Botchan" tourist train that runs through Matsuyama.

The 19 living quarters of Yamatoya Besso are named for flowers and are spacious suites of two to three adjoining rooms with private bathrooms. A *kaiseki* dinner of several courses and breakfast are served in guests' rooms and feature the freshest produce of the season as well as fish from the Inland Sea. The attention to detail and charming, thoughtful services make this a truly pampering spa experience. The two indoor male and female spring baths connect to open-air baths. Ladies can select from a choice of cotton kimono designs. The outpouring of bath-side beer is plentiful, and the offering of ionized drinking water post-bath is much appreciated. The indulgence of a soupçon of sushi just before a night of sublime repose is a small yet inspired gesture.

Address: 2-27 Sagiya-cho, Dogo, Matsuyama-shi, Ehime-ken 790-0836, Japan. **Tel:** 81 (0)89 931 7771. **Fax:** 81 (0)89 931 7775. **Website:** www.yamatoyabesso.com. **E-mail:** info@yamatoyabesso.com. **Rooms:** 19. **Access:** 1 hr flight from Haneda to Matsuyama Airport by ANA and 30 min to Dogo by taxi.

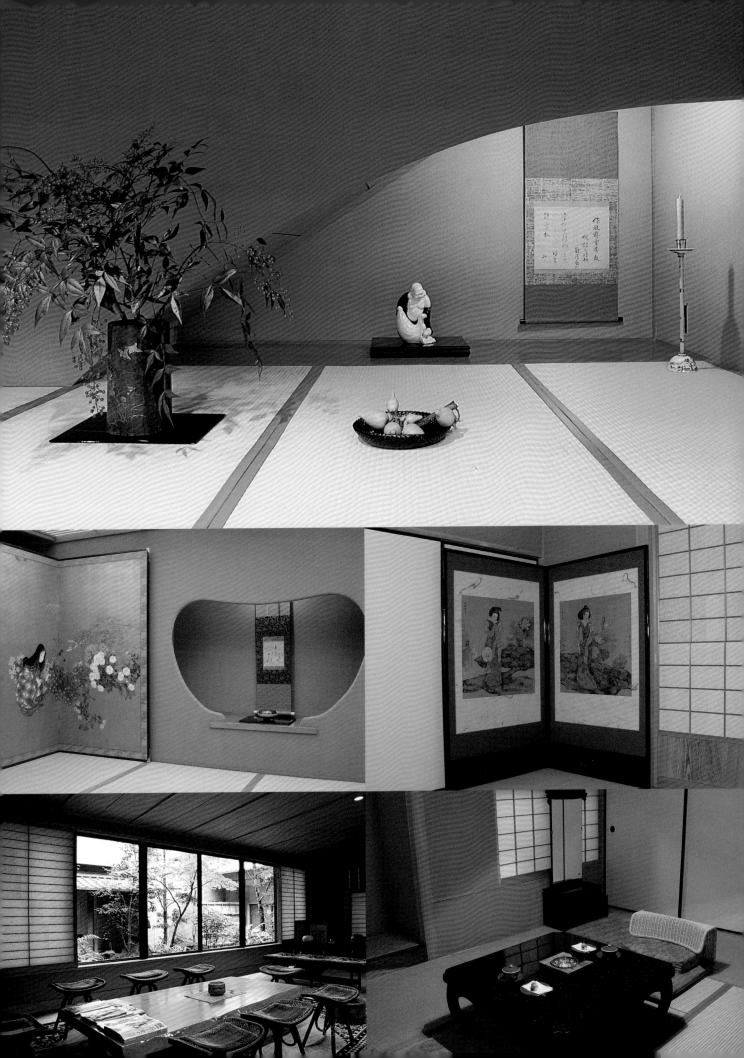

Murata 無量塔 Yufuin, Oita

In the language of Buddhism, *murata* signifies "immeasurable hospitality." Host Koji Fujibayashi has created a "petit" onsen ryokan, a comforting space for what his Japanese and English website calls a "soul trip."

It is a bit of a journey to reach the pastoral highland plateau setting of Murata and Yufuin Onsen on the east coast of Kyushu, about an hour's drive from Oita Airport.

Tucked among trees at the foot of Mount Yufudake, Yufuin remains a quiet onsen village, a contrast to the tourist attraction of neighboring Beppu Onsen, the largest onsen resort city in all of Japan, acclaimed for having a remarkable volume of natural spring waters. Yufuin was little known until the early 1990s, when clever innkeepers such as Mr Fujibayashi recognized the fresh appeal of a cozy getaway rather than the vast impersonal space of resorts catering to tour groups and conventions.

Murata is a collection of rugged, century-old farmhouses that have been preserved and relocated from Niigata and from Shiga, near Kyoto. Several of the eight independent cottages, private apartments, are *gassho zukuri*, multi-storied fairytale farmhouses of pampas thatched roofs. Mr Fujibayashi has taken these romantic residential shells and transformed their interiors into open, airy spaces of Western and Eastern comfort. In the 130-year-old "Meiji" farmhouse, for instance, the second-floor silkworm room has been removed to transform the interior space into a grand room with a lofty ceiling of glorious wooden beams.

Each villa has three to five rooms, a large living room and a private hot spring *ofuro* ("bathtub") of stone. The bathing area is walled in natural cypress, and there are picture windows for viewing the changes of the season. There are Le Corbusier sofas, Persian carpets, antiques, Western beds, down comforters, ample reading light, as well as Japanese tatami rooms for those who prefer a futon.

Dinner and breakfast are served and prepared over the hearth in the Saihidou dining room in the main building. Sweet bean or jam buns, *omanju*, might be steaming. *Zaru-soba*, a bamboo basket of buckwheat noodles with tangy soy sauce, could be served for lunch. The restaurant is open to the public from 11:30 to 9:30 and offers a variety of set menus. Tan's Bar is a sophisticated space for tea, or a favorite sake or scotch. The lighting is indirect, intimate. The B-speak café is a relatively new addition. There is a chocolate shop, Chocolatier Zo and a next-door museum, Artegio, with changing exhibitions and pieces from the collections of ryokan owner Fujibayashi.

Gaze at fluffy cloud forms at play on the mountain peak, look into the dance of flames in the warming fireplace, do nothing but soak in soft waters, meditating on travels of one's soul.

Address: 1264-2 Kawakami, Yufuin-cho, Oita-gun, Oita-ken 879-51, Japan. **Tel:** 81 (0)977 84 5000. **Fax:** 81 (0)977 84 5001. **Website:** www.sansou-murata.com. **E-mail:** murata1992@sansou-murata.com. **Rooms:** 8. **Access:** 1 hr 40 min flight from Haneda to Oita Airport and 1 hr from Oita Airport to Yufuin by taxi or bus.

Miyazaki Ryokan 宮崎旅館　Unzen, Nagasaki

Mists mysterious and sulfur-rich, sourced from an active volcano, Mount Fugen.
Paths of stone meander for strolls in study of the earth's bewildering energies.
Miyazaki Ryokan is a multi-story lodging plopped amidst the steaming mineral
waters of Unzen, about 100 kilometers southeast of Nagasaki in Kyushu.

During the Edo Period (1603–1868) Nagasaki received a rare few outsiders for the
strict purposes of trade or diplomacy. Perhaps it was these worldly travelers who
sparked a national passion for golf—Unzen opened Japan's first golf course in 1913.
In 1934, Unzen was designated as the first national park in Japan and was named for
the volcanic chain, Mount Unzen. The Hells, *jigoku*, of Unzen Spa boil with geothermal
activity. Women in bonnets dip crates of eggs into the waters and sell onsen *tamago*,
hot-spring-boiled eggs, to passersby.

Since its opening in 1929, Miyazaki Ryokan has been managed by three generations of smiling Miyazaki women: Sueko, her daughter, Michiko, and now her grand-
daughter-in-law, Chizuko. In their obi-wrapped kimono, these three women personify
the long Japanese traditions of artful entertaining. As *okami*, they oversee design,
service, flower arranging and meal preparation. They give the unique personal attention that makes guests feel pampered, significant. Emperor Hirohito once stayed here.

At 700 meters above sea level, Unzen is refreshing throughout the year. The hills
of the Shimabara Peninsula are a mosaic of yellows, rusts, sage and khaki in autumn.
Frosts whiten the vistas in winter. In April and May as many as 1,500 bushes at Miyazaki
Ryokan astound in blushing azalea rose and pink and purple and red. Throughout the
year the national park is a bird sanctuary, but early summer is a particularly popular
bird time. The glass walls of the ryokan overlook a Japanese garden of white stone,
sculptural rock formations, ornamental *matsu* pine, stone stupa and splashing waterfalls.

This is a big inn of 98 rooms, some with Western beds, more typically in Japanese style with *shoji* paper doors, tatami floors, low lacquer tables, perhaps a hand-painted lacquer *cha-dansu* for keeping tea cups and saucers. There are two marble indoor hot springs, two rock-rimmed open-air baths for full-moon viewing and three family-sized baths. There is usually a time limit when reserving a more private family bath. There is also a sauna, a coffee lounge, meeting rooms and banquet room as well as a place for singing karaoke.

Meals are taken in the dining room. There could be shrimp or a fan of wafer-thin *fugu*, blowfish, served with a tiny lime. Western breakfast is available. Only a five-minute taxi ride away, Japan's historic links are remarkably affordable.

Fumes of sulfur, plumes of gauzy vapor weaving in and out of pines and blossoms red. Mesmerizing soothing waters. Best to book three months in anticipation.

Address: Unzen, Kohama-cho, Minami-Takagi-gun, Nagasaki-ken 854-062, Japan. **Tel:** 81 (0)957 73 3331. **Fax:** 81 (0)957 73 2313. **Website:** www.miyazaki-ryokan.co.jp. **E-mail:** unzen@miyazaki-ryokan.co.jp. **Rooms:** 98. **Access:** 1 hr 30 min flight from Tokyo to Nagasaki Airport, 1 hr 30 min from Nagasaki Airport to Miyazaki Ryokan by taxi or bus.

Yusai 優彩 Kurokawa Onsen, Kumamoto

Reflections serene, surreal. Towering trees on warm, still waters. The contented smile of a welcoming stone deity. The glow of lantern light and the fascinating dynamic of shadow play. Humble imagery enchants. It is enough, more than enough. Life in the 21st century is heavy with contrived, complicated pleasures. The appeal of the un-assuming country village of Minami-Oguri-cho, its Kurokawa hot spring waters and an inn such as Yusai is a determination to showcase the natural, the authentic.

In part due to its remote simplicity, Kurokawa Onsen has become one of Japan's most popular onsen towns. In order to reach the magical world of Yusai it is neces-sary to travel by plane and train and taxi. Kumamoto is located in western Kyushu, an hour and 40-minute flight from Tokyo's Haneda Airport. The closest station to Yusai, Aso is another hour away by local train, then there is a 30-minute car ride to Kurokawa Onsen.

The owner of Yusai, Jyunichi Takashima, well understands what brings travelers from afar: soothing mineral-rich waters beyond compare. With this in mind, he has helped to establish a community ticketing system that allows guests to "*rotenburo* hop" among the area's 26 ryokan onsen. With 58 rooms, Yusai is the largest onsen resort in the area.

Upon arrival, the exterior of Yusai may seem yet another replica of a big and Western and characterless hotel, but the inner sanctum of Yusai reflects a very different sensibility. Lighting is soft, judiciously utilizing spots to shed just enough illumination to direct guests' attention to walls of Japanese cypress, bamboo or pointillist statements in stone. Floors of tatami matting are open and uncluttered. Some rooms have Western beds, yet all décor is minimalist, understated, colored in rough rock grays, reed neutrals.

Yusai's luxurious onsen, Chikurin-no-Yu, must be one of the most dramatically stunning in all of Japan. Bathers soak cares, distractions, aches and tension away in the mist of a green, graceful bamboo forest. It is as if spa-goers have surreptitiously entered the world of an ancient Japanese watercolor. Yusai has four communal indoor hot springs, two for men, two for women, two *rotenburo* and two family hot springs for those who wish to reserve a more private pool.

Dinner and breakfast may be eaten in guests' rooms or in the dining room. The menu is very au courant, offering health-conscious samplings of mountain vegetables, bamboo shoots, and mushrooms, and as many as 10 to 15 delicate taste marvels are simultaneously served.

As day turns to night, guests' concerns are centered on place. At Yusai, there are seats up on the roof… for viewing sunset in the mountains, in the forests cedar. Or, there are waters warm, inviting relief, amid gold-lit bamboo.

Address: Kurokawa Onsen, Minami Oguri-machi, Aso-gun, Kumamoto-ken 869-2402, Japan. **Tel:** 81 (0)967 44 0111. **Fax:** 81 (0)967 44 0115. **Website:** www.yusai.com. **Rooms:** 58. **Access:** 1 hr 40 min flight from Haneda to Kumamoto Airport, 1 hr to Aso Station by local train and 30 min to Kurokawa Onsen by taxi.

Gajoen 雅叙苑 Makizono, Kagoshima

A return to a pure earth. The transcendent peace of fewer things. A heightened awareness of the *wabi-sabi* beauty of nature's rhythms. Living in the country or living on the farm is far from poetically easy, but its day-to-day elegance and truth come from the primal necessity to observe nature.

Far to the south of Kyushu, beside a river, in a forest and overlooking mountains, a former banker and his wife have recreated a thatched-roof hamlet. Gajoen, sourced from the sulfur- and iron-rich Myoken Onsen in Makizono, north of Kagoshima, is probably the most highly sought after ryokan in all of Japan.

In the 1970s Tateo Tajima quit his local banking job, purchased a small inn and took to the land. He collected, transplanted and reassembled thatched roof houses; he planted bamboo and flowers and with his wife Etsuko, sought to return to a quintessential time.

Today guests at Gajoen share the gardens and stone walkways with pecking and strutting chickens. Depending on the season, there may be *daikon* hanging to dry, a numinous fog floating among the trees. There are only 10 thatched or terra cotta roofed cottage rooms, each giving guests very private farm-style living space. Ceilings are of wood, walls of plaster, a main room floored in fragrant rush tatami. Vessels for a variety of purposes, vases, bowls and pots are made of bamboo.

Eight of the 10 rooms have private *rotenburo*. From the four communal *rotenburo*, bathers can listen to the music of the river. The mens and women's indoor communal baths are of rugged rock and concrete. On the way to the river, there are an additional two family baths for couple-sharing or the carefree water-play of children.

An organic farm-fresh dinner is served in guests' cottages. There could be sukiyaki of shaved beef, shiitake and shimeji mushrooms, green onions and spring

chrysanthemums or broiled *ayu*, the sweet white river fish or a light crisp vegetarian tempura. After the roosters crow, a fruits-of-the-farm breakfast is served in a spacious thatched lodge.

Mr Tajima's latest project is Tenkuh no Mori, a nearby hilltop forest haven of five villas, each with its own open-air hot spring bath. This exclusive retreat is about a 10-minute drive from Gajoen. Its bathtub views of the Kirishima Mountains are enchanting, perhaps without equal in all of Japan. This stunning hideaway is the Tajimas' "work in progress," so only a few of the villas may be available for overnight stays, but guests can now reserve, for an additional fee, picnic lunches of ham or pork cutlet sandwiches, fresh fruit and thermos hot coffee.

The Tajimas speak little English, but their service is full of smiles. The innkeepers understand the primitive pleasure of nature pared to its essence. Gajoen is so in demand it would be wise to make plans a year in advance. In late autumn—the trees, the skies, cool air, warm water—Gajoen is pure bliss.

Address: 4230 Kubota, Makizono-cho, Aira-gun, Kagoshima-ken 899-6507, Japan. **Tel:** 81 (0)995 77 2114. **Fax:** 81 (0)995 77 2203. **Rooms:** 10. **Access:** 1 hr 50 min flight from Haneda to Kagoshima Airport and 20 min to Myoken Onsen by taxi.

Ryokan List

Araya Totoan
Yamashiro Onsen, Kaga-shi, Ishikawa-ken 922-0242, Japan. Tel: 81 (0)761 77 0010. Fax: 81 (0)761 77 0008. Website: www.araya-totoan.com. E-mail: info@araya-totoan.com. Rooms: 20. Access: 1 hr flight from Haneda to Komatsu Airport and 30 min from Airport to Yamashiro by taxi.

Atami Sekitei
6-17 Wada-cho, Atami-shi, Shizuoka-ken 413-0024, Japan. Tel: 81 (0)557 83 2841. Fax: 81 (0)557 82 2840. Website: www.sekitei.co.jp. E-mail: sekitei@sekitei.co.jp. Rooms: Sekitei 29, Sakuragaoka-Saryo 10. Access: 50 min from Tokyo to Atami Station by Tokaido Shinkansen and 5 min to Sekitei by taxi.

Bankyu Ryokan
749 Yunishigawa, Kuriyama-mura, Shioya-gun, Tochigi-ken 321-2601, Japan. Tel: 81 (0)288 98 0011. Fax: 81 (0)288 98 0666. Website: www.bankyu.co.jp. E-mail: info@bankyu.co.jp. Rooms: 45. Access: 2 hrs from Tobu Asakusa to Yunishigawa Onsen Station by Tobu Aizu-kinugawa line and 30 min to Yunishigawa by bus.

Gajoen
4230 Kubota, Makizono-cho, Aira-gun, Kagoshima-ken 899-6507, Japan. Tel: 81 (0)995 77 2114. Fax: 81 (0)995 77 2203. Rooms: 10. Access: 1 hr 50 min flight from Haneda to Kagoshima Airport and 20 min to Myoken Onsen by taxi.

Gora Kadan
1300 Gora, Hakone-machi, Ashigarashimo-gun, Kanagawa-ken 250-0408, Japan. Tel: 81 (0)460 2 3331. Fax: 81 (0)460 2 3334. Website: www.gorakadan.com. E-mail: info@gorakadan.com. Rooms: 37. Access: 40 min from Tokyo to Odawara Station by Tokaido Shinkansen and 30 min drive to Gora by taxi.

Hiiragiya
Oike-kado, Fuya-cho, Nakakyo-ku, Kyoto 604-8094, Japan. Tel: 81 (0)75 221 1136. Fax: 81 (0)75 221 1139. Website: www.hiiragiya.co.jp. E-mail: info@hiiragiya.co.jp. Rooms: 30. Access: 2 hrs from Tokyo to Kyoto Station by Tokaido Shinkansen and 15 min to Hiiragiya by taxi.

Houshi
Awazu Onsen, Komatsu-shi, Ishikawa-ken 923-0326, Japan. Tel: 81 (0)761 65 1111. Fax: 81 (0)761 65 1115. Website: www.ho-shi.co.jp. E-mail: ho-shi@ho-shi.co.jp. Rooms: 74. Access: 1 hr flight from Haneda to Komatsu Airport and 15 min to Awazu Onsen by taxi.

Kayotei
Higashi-machi, Yamanaka-cho, Enuma-gun, Ishikawa-ken 922-0114, Japan. Tel: 81(0)761 78 1410. Fax: 81 (0)761 78 1121. Rooms: 10. Access: 1 hr flight from Haneda to Komatsu Airport and 30 min to Yamanaka by taxi.

Kona Besso
31 Kona, Izu-Nagaoka-cho, Tagata-gun, Shizuoka-ken 410-0022, Japan. Tel: 81 (0)559 48 1225. Fax: 81 (0)559 47 1225. Website: www.konabesso.com. Rooms: 8. Access: 1 hr from Tokyo to Mishima by Tokaido Shinkansen and 30 min to Nagaoka by train or by taxi.

Kikusuiro
1130 Takabatake-cho, Nara-shi, Nara-ken 630-8301, Japan. Tel: 81 (0)742 23 2001. Fax: 81 (0)742 26 0025. Rooms: 13. Access: 1 hr flight from Haneda to Itami Airport by ANA or JAL, 1 hr by limousine bus to Kintetsu Nara Station and 5 min to Kikusuiro by taxi.

Kuramure
2-685 Asarigawa Onsen, Otaru-shi, Hokkaido 047-0154, Japan. Tel: 81 (0)134 51 5151. Fax: 81 (0)134 51 5000. Website: www.kuramure.com. E-mail: international@kuramure.com. Rooms: 19. Access: 1 hr 30 min flight from Haneda to Chitose Airport, 1 hr to Otaru-Chikuko by JR train and 5 min to Kuramure by taxi.

Miyazaki Ryokan
Unzen, Kohama-cho, Minami-Takaki-gun, Nagasaki-ken 854-0621, Japan. Tel: 81 (0)957 73 3331. Fax: 81 (0)957 73 2313. Website: www.miyazaki-ryokan.co.jp. E-mail: unzen@miyazaki-ryokan.co.jp. Rooms: 98. Access: 1 hr 30 min flight from Tokyo to Nagasaki Airport, 1 hr 30 min from Nagasaki Airport to Miyazaki Ryokan by taxi or bus.

Mukaitaki
Higashiyama-cho, Aizu-Wakamatsu-shi, Fukushima-ken 965-0814, Japan. Tel: 81 (0)242 27 7501. Fax: 81 (0)242 28 0939. Website: www.mukaitaki.com. E-mail: ryokan@mukaitaki.com. Rooms: 24. Access: 2 hrs 30 min from Tokyo to Aizu-Wakamatsu Station via Kooriyama by Tohoku Shinkansen and Banetsu-Saisen and 15 min to Higashiyama Onsen by taxi.

Murata
1264-2 Kawakami, Yufuin-cho, Oita-gun, Oita-ken 879-51, Japan. Tel: 81 (0)977 84 5000. Fax: 81 (0)977 84 5001. Website: www.sansou-murata.com. E-mail: murata1992@sansou-murata.com. Rooms: 8. Access: 1 hr 40 min flight from Haneda to Oita Airport and 1 hr from Oita Airport to Yufuin by taxi or bus.

Ryugon
79 Sakado, Minami-Uonuma-shi, Niigata-ken 949-6611, Japan. Tel: 81 (0)25 772 3470. Fax: 81 (0)25 772 2124. Website: www.ryugon.co.jp. E-mail: info@ryugon.co.jp. Rooms: 32. Access: (1) 1 hr 20 min from Ueno to Echigo-Yuzawa Station by Jyoetsu-Shinkansen and 20 min to Ryugon by taxi. (2) 2 hrs 45 min drive from Nerima IC in Tokyo to Minami-Uonuma IC by Kanetsu Jidoshado and 10 min drive to Ryugon.

Sanraku
206 Yumoto, Nasu-machi, Nasu-gun, Tochigi-ken 325-0301, Japan. Tel: 81 (0)287 76 3010. Fax: 81 (0)287 76 4638. Website: www.e-sanraku.com. E-mail: sanraku@peach.ocn.ne.jp. Rooms: 38. Access: (1) 1 hr 15 min from Tokyo to Nasu-Shiobara Station by Tohoku Shinkansen and 20 min to Sanraku by taxi. (2) 2 hrs drive from Nerima IC to Nasu IC by Tohoku-Jidosha-Do and 20 min drive to Sanraku on Route 17.

Saryo Soen
Akiu-cho, Taihaku-ku, Sendai-shi, Miyagi-ken 982-0241, Japan. Tel: 81 (0)22 398 2311. Fax: 81 (0)22 398 2144. Rooms: 26. Access: 1 hr 40 min from Tokyo to Sendai Station by Tohoku Shinkansen and 40 min to Saryo Soen by taxi.

Seikoro Inn
Tonyamachi, Gojo Sagaru, Higashiyama-ku, Kyoto 605-0907, Japan. Tel: 81 (0)75 561 0771. Fax: 81 (0)75 541 5481. Website: www.seikoro.com. E-mail: yoyaku@seikoro.com. Rooms: 22. Access: 2 hrs 30 min from Tokyo to Kyoto Station by Tokaido Shinkansen and 10 min to Seikoro by taxi.

Seiryuso
2-2 Kochi, Shimoda-shi, Shizuoka-ken 415-0011, Japan. Tel: 81 (0)558 22 1361. Fax: 81 (0)558 23 2066. Website: www.seiryuso.co.jp. E-mail: info@seiryuso.co.jp. Rooms: 26. Access: 2 hrs 30 min from Tokyo to Shimoda Station by Izu Express Line and 5 min to Seiryuso by taxi.

Sekitei
Miyahama Onsen, Ohno-cho, Saeki-gun, Hiroshima-ken 739-0454, Japan. Tel: 81 (0)829 55 0601. Fax: 81 (0)829 55 0603. Website: www.sekitei.to. E-mail: info@sekitei.to. Rooms: 10. Access: 1 hr 30 min flight from Haneda to Hiroshima Airport and 30 min to Miyahama by taxi.

Senjyuan
Tanigawa-Nishidaira, Minakami-cho, Tone-gun, Gunma-ken 379-1619, Japan. Tel: 81 (0)278 20 4141. Fax: 81 (0)278 72 1860. Website: www.ryokan-tanigawa.com. E-mail: senjyuan@ryokan-tanigawa.com. Rooms: 18. Access: (1) 1 hr 50 min drive from Nerima IC to Minakami IC by Kanetsu-Jidoshado and 5 min drive to Senjyuan. (2) 1 hr 20 min from Tokyo to Jyomo Kogen Station by Jyoetsu Shinkansen and 30 min to Senjyuan by taxi.

Tsubaki
Oku-Yugawara, Yugawara-cho, Ashigarashimo-gun, Kanagawa-ken 259-0314, Japan. Tel: 81 (0)465 63 3333. Fax: 81 (0)465 63 6640. Website: www.tsubaki.net. E-mail: kaiseki@tsubaki.net. Rooms: 29. Access: (1) 50 min from Tokyo to Atami Station by Tokaido Shinkansen and 10 min to Tsubaki by taxi. (2) 2 hrs drive from Tokyo to Oku-Yugawara through Tomei Kosoku, Odawara-Atsugi Doro and Manazuru-Doro.

Tsuru-no-Yu
Tazawako-machi, Senboku-gun, Akita-ken 014-1204, Japan. Tel: 81 (0)187 46 2139. Fax: 81 (0)187 46 2761. Website: www.tsurunoyu.com. Rooms: 35. Access: (1) 1 hr flight from Haneda to Akita Airport and 2 hrs drive to Nyuto Onsen by taxi or limousine bus. (2) 3 hrs from Tokyo to Tazawako by Akita Shinkansen and 30 min to Nyuto Onsen by taxi.

Yamatoya Besso
2-27 Sagiya-cho, Dogo, Matsuyama-shi, Ehime-ken 790-0836, Japan. Tel: 81 (0)89 931 7771. Fax: 81 (0)89 931 7775. Website: www.yamatoyabesso.com. E-mail: info@yamatoyabesso.com. Rooms: 19. Access: 1 hr flight from Haneda to Matsuyama Airport by ANA and 30 min to Dogo by taxi.

Yagyu-no-Sho
1116-6, Shuzenji, Shuzenji-cho, Tagata-gun, Shizuoka-ken 410-2416, Japan. Tel: 81 (0)558 72 4126. Fax: 81 (0)558 72 5212. Website: www.yagyu-no-sho.com. E-mail: info@yagyu-no-sho.com. Rooms: 16. Access: 1 hr from Tokyo to Mishima Station by Tokaido Shinkansen and 30 min to Shuzenji by train or by taxi.

Yumoto Choza
Fukuchi Onsen, Kamitakara-mura, Kichijyou-gun, Gifu-ken 506-1434, Japan. Tel: 81 (0)578 9 0099. Fax: 81 (0)578 9 2010. Rooms: 32. Access: 2 hrs 30 min from Tokyo to Matsumoto Station by Express Train Azusa and 1 hr to Fukuchi Onsen by taxi or bus.

Yusai
Kurokawa Onsen, Minami Oguri-machi, Aso-gun, Kumamoto-ken 869-2402, Japan. Tel: 81 (0)967 44 0111. Fax: 81 (0)967 44 0115. Website: www.yusai.com. Rooms: 58. Access: 1 hr 40 min flight from Haneda to Kumamoto Airport, 1 hr to Aso Station by local train and 30 min to Kurokawa Onsen by taxi.

Wanosato
1682 Miya-mura, Ohno-gun, Gifu-ken, 509-3538, Japan. Tel: 81 (0)577 53 2321. Fax: 81 (0)577 53 3220. Rooms: 8. Access: 2 hrs from Tokyo to Nagoya Station by Tokaido Shinkansen, 2 hrs 30 min to Takayama Station by local train and 20 min to Wanosato by taxi.

Akihiko Seki wishes to thank all ryokan for
their warm hospitality and cooperation. A
special thank you to Asako for her assistance
and companionship.

Elizabeth Heilman Brooke wishes to thank the
gentle friends who have shared their knowledge
of Japanese history, architecture, art and entertaining with her. A bow of appreciation to Jim,
loving guide on a lifetime of extraordinary journeys.

Published in 2005 by Tuttle Publishing, an imprint
of Periplus Editions (HK) Ltd, with editorial offices
at 130, Joo Seng Road, #06–01/03, Olivine
Building, Singapore 368357.

ISBN: 0-8048-3671-X
Printed in Singapore.

Distributed by
North America, Latin America and Europe
Tuttle Publishing, 364 Innovation Drive,
North Clarendon, VT 05759-9436
tel: (802) 773 8930, fax: (802) 773 6993
email: info@tuttlepublishing.com
www.tuttlepublishing.com

Japan
Tuttle Publishing, Yaekari Building,
3F 5-4-12 Osaki, Shinagawa-ku,
Tokyo 141-0032
tel: (03) 5437 0171, fax: (03) 5437 0755
email: tuttle-sales@gol.com

Asia Pacific
Berkeley Books Pte Ltd
130 Joo Seng Road #06-01/03,
Singapore 368357
tel: (65) 6280 1330, fax: (65) 6280 6290
email: inquiries@periplus.com.sg
www.periplus.com

Indonesia
PT Java Books Indonesia
Jl Kelapa Gading Kirana,
Blok A-14/17, Jakarta 14240
tel: (62 21) 451 5351, fax: (62 21) 453 4987
email: cs@javabooks.co.id

10 09 08 07 06
6 5 4 3 2